The Sun & Moon Guide to

Eating Through Literature and Art

Edited and with a Note
by Douglas Messerli

LOS ANGELES
SUN & MOON PRESS
1994

Sun & Moon Press
A Program of The Contemporary Arts Educational Project, Inc.
a nonprofit corporation
6026 Wilshire Boulevard, Los Angeles, California 90036

First published as a trade cloth edition by Sun & Moon Press, 1994
10 9 8 7 6 5 4 3 2 1
©1994 by Sun & Moon Press
See "Sources and Permissions" at
the back of this book for all other permissions and copyrights.
All rights reserved

This book was made possible, in part, through an operational grant from the
Andrew W. Mellon Foundation, and through contributions to
The Contemporary Arts Educational Project, Inc.,
a nonprofit corporation

Cover: Collage by Katie Messborn of
A. Rodchenko's photograph, *Factory Kitchen,* 1932
reproduced upon his *Pure red paint,* 1921.
Design: Katie Messborn and Guy Bennett
Typography: Guy Bennett

LIBRARY OF CONGRESS CATALOGING IN PUBLICATION DATA
Messerli, Douglas, ed. [1947]
The Sun & Moon Guide to eating through literature and art / edited and
with a note by Douglas Messerli.
p. cm
Includes bibliographical references.
ISBN: 1-55713-178-3 : $29.95
1. Cookery. 2. Food in art. 3. Food in literature.
I. Messerli, Douglas, 1947–   . II. Title: Sun & Moon guide to
eating through literature and art. III. Title: Guide to eating
through literature and art.
TX714.S856   1994
641'.01'3—dc20
94-34013
CIP

Printed in Korea by Sun Print.

A NOTE

IN LATE 1988 I sent out letters to several authors of international significance, asking them for a NewYear's contribution to Sun & Moon Press in the form of a recipe. Certainly, I had seen collections of author's and artist's recipes before, but I felt the selection of writers that I had asked would assure a wide range of responses. And that is precisely what I received. Well known gourmet John Cage sent me, on one of his famous "Message and Reply Note-o-grams," a recipe for Pesto Sauce; Ruth Prawer Jhabvala shared her "Jhabvala's Fish Pilao"; Mary McCarthy described a delicious "Tomates à la crème"; Paul Auster told the story of his Onion Pie; Ernesto Cardenal sent me a text, in Spanish, about corn by José Coronel Urtecho; Václav Havel, long before his rise to the presidency of the Czech Republic, provided the makings of a "Beefsteak with a Sweet-Sour Gravy"; and dozens of others sent along their culinary favorites.

For all the range of food and gastronomic memories—perhaps *because* of the range—the writings did not cohere for me as a book, at least not a Sun & Moon book. Instead, I put these recipes away in files, and let the idea of the book sink into the far recesses of my mind. Yet they never left my memory, and a few years later it came to me that perhaps the problem with this potential book was the fact that I was not seeking a book of recipes, but a book about food, about the very act of eating.

Immediately upon reconceiving this project, I began to encounter passages about food in nearly every book I read. Upon reading *The Great Fire of London* by Jacques Roubaud, published by my friend John O'Brien, I discovered the remarkable "Law of Butter Croissants"; Robert Walser's writing was a virtual cornucopia of eating delights; our own Sun & Moon publications such as Jens Bjørneboe's *The Bird Lovers* and Charley George's *Sunday's Ending Too Soon* were filled with descriptions of food. I began remembering passages from my college reading. And before long, I started seeing images of food in every art book I picked up. Food, so it appears, was coming to me; and I was gaining a great deal of weight in the process. There seemed only one way out: release, to publish the book I had years before begun.

The result is the cacaphony of words and images before you, a guide—in the very broadest sense—to what people put into their mouths (or refuse to, in the cases of Kathy Acker, Eugène Ionesco, and Isaac Bashevis Singer). *Bon appétit.*

—Douglas Messerli

Bill of Fare

DEPRIVATION, STRANGE TASTES

BREAKFAST

SPICES, SOUPS, SAUCES, LIGHT MEALS, LUNCHES

REUNIONS AND TEA

ENTRÉES

MEMORIES, CIGARS, LIQUORS AND LATE NIGHT SNACKS

Deprivation
Strange Tastes

Eleanor Antin, *A Refusal* from *The 8 Temptations* (1972)

Champagne is Not Allowed

KATHY ACKER

I WOULD LOVE to send you my favorite recipe. (As I remember, that's what you asked for). However, since my marriage broke up, about ten years ago, I haven't cooked for anyone, except for the most minimal of pasta dishes, and barely for myself. I tend to eat raw vegetables, yogurt, and smoked fish, or else to eat out. I can't imagine that a list of inexpensive London restaurants would interest anyone. If it is of any concern, how could it be, my favorite foods are raw fish, especially raw sea urchin, and then just about anything raw, though I don't eat red meats. And when I can afford it and especially when I can't, if the dollar disintegrates anymore we'll all have to assassinate Reagan, champagne. Since I body-build rather seriously amateur-style, my diet is limited by a mean and vicious trainer, Jamie the Beast, who torments me for fun: champagne is not allowed. Maybe that's why I love it.

Potatoes Can't Think

ISAAC B. SINGER

A memory by Douglas Messerli

WHEN I LIVED in New York, I often visited my former teacher, Isaac Bashevis Singer, either in his West Side apartment or, since Singer—opposed to the killing of animals—was a vegetarian, in a nearby dairy bar.

Isaac Singer loved unusual stories, particularly those of the supernatural or that involved strange phenomena. So I often came armed with such stories. One time I asked had he read about the recent experiments scientists have been conducting on plants. "They hook them up to lie detectors," I reported, "and they've discovered that the plants react when spoken to, particularly when they're threatened. A scientist produces a large knife, and the plant goes wild—according to the reading on the lie detector. Even if the scientist just says I'm going to kill the plant, it evidently has a horrible reaction. One scientist reported that he was going to cut another plant, and the tree, hooked up to the apparatus, went crazy."

Singer thought about this silently for a long while, then drew a deep breath, and in his strong Yiddish accent pronounced: "I don't believe a potato can think!" He was silent for a few more seconds. "Besides...if it could...what would I eat?"

Starvation

EUGÈNE IONESCO

I DECIDED TO EAT no more fruit, or butter, or carrots, or cheese, or salad, or radishes, or mushrooms. I grew thinner and weaker, I became dull and dejected. My pains shifted; my right shoulder began to ache, then my left, then both at once; my fingers grew numb, my headaches started up again, together with dental neuralgia. I probably sweated too much, I had caught a chill. I drank scarcely any water. My kidneys, like parched earth, grew hard; I found it painful to bend. I had an ache like a long bruise beneath my ribs. I was so afraid of food that I stopped eating. Of course I grew still thinner, visibly so. But I did not become any lighter, on the contrary: heaviness took possession of me. My legs gave way under the weight of a bent body, of mere bones, I had cramp in my calves, and my feet were frozen.

I still maintained a certain activity. Some automatic reactions, some reflexes that had not yet completely broken down went on functioning pointlessly and ineffectively, like the limbs of a beheaded frog. I still went wandering over hill and dale, dragging myself along. Now it wearied me to breathe. The air was as heavy as my arms, and my briefcase was like lead. At every step I needed to overcome a stubborn resistance that was invisible and yet material.

I could no longer endure noises: everything grated on my ears, every voice, even a child's, seemed to me a shrill, piercing cry that rent me physically. I discerned sounds as though through a solid element, amplified and coarsened. This distorted my estimate of distances, which my failing eyesight strove hard to correct. Then cries, like knives, seemed to shatter my ear-drums; I heard leaves fall, as heavy as stones; the rustle of trees seemed to tear the air close to me.

Translated by Jean Stewart

Half-Decayed Vegetables & "Uneatable" Cheese

FRANZ KAFKA

...HIS SISTER, nearly fully dressed, opened the door from the hall and peered in. She did not see him at once, yet when she caught sight of him under the sofa—well, he had to be somewhere, he couldn't have flown away, could he?—she was so startled that without being able to help it she slammed the door shut again. But as if regretting her behavior she opened the door again immediately and came in on tiptoe, as if she were visiting an invalid or even a stranger. Gregor had pushed his head forward to the very edge of the sofa and watched her. Would she notice that he had left the milk standing, and not for lack of hunger, and would she bring in some other kind of food more to his taste? If she did not do it of her own accord, he would rather starve than draw her attention to the fact, although he felt a wild impulse to dart out from under the sofa, throw himself at her feet and beg her for something to eat. But his sister at once noticed, with surprise, that the bowl was still full, except for a little milk that had been spilt all around

it, she lifted it immediately, not with her bare hands, true, but with a cloth and carried it away. Gregor was wildly curious to know what she would bring instead, and made various speculations about it. Yet what she actually did next, in the goodness of her heart, he could never have guessed at. To find out what he liked she brought him a whole selec-

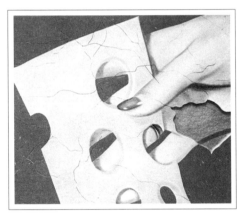

James Rosenquist, *Silhouette* II, (1962)

tion of food, all set out on an old newspaper. There were old, half-decayed vegetables, bones from last night's supper covered with a white sauce that had thickened; some raisins and almonds; a piece of cheese that Gregor would have called uneatable two days ago; a dry roll of bread, a buttered roll, and a roll both buttered and salted. Besides all that, she set down again the same bowl, into

which she had poured some water, and which was apparently to be reserved for his exclusive use. And with fine tact, knowing that Gregor would not eat in her presence, she withdrew quickly and even turned the key, to let him understand that he could take his ease as much as he liked. Gregor's legs all whizzed towards the food. His wounds must have healed completely, moreover, for he felt no disability, which amazed him and made him reflect how more than a month ago he had cut one finger a little with a knife and had still suffered pain from the wound only the day before yesterday. Am I less sensitive now? he thought, and sucked greedily at the cheese, which above all the other edibles attracted him at once and strongly. One after another and with tears of satisfaction in his eyes he quickly devoured the cheese, the vegetables and the sauce; the fresh food, on the other hand, had no charms for him, he could not even stand the smell of it and actually dragged away to some little distance the things he could eat. He had long finished his meal and was only lying lazily on the same spot when his sister turned the key slowly as a sign for him to retreat.

Earth

GABRIEL GARCÍA MÁRQUEZ

ALTHOUGH SHE SEEMED expansive and cordial, she had a solitary character and an impenetrable heart. She was a splendid adolescent with long and firm bones, but she still insisted on using the small wooden rocking chair with which she had arrived at the house, reinforced many times and with the arms gone. No one had discovered that even at that age she still had the habit of sucking her finger. That was why she would not lose an opportunity to lock herself in the bathroom and had acquired the habit of sleeping with her face to the wall. On rainy afternoons, embroidering with a group of friends on the begonia porch, she would lose the thread of the conversation and a tear of nostalgia would salt her palate when she saw the strips of damp earth and the piles of mud that the earthworms had pushed up in the garden. Those secret tastes, defeated in the past by oranges and rhubarb, broke out into an irrepressible urge when she began to weep. She went back to eating earth. The first time she did it almost out of curiosity, sure that the bad taste would be the best cure for the temptation. And, in fact, she could not bear the earth in her mouth. But she persevered, overcome by the growing anxiety, and little by little she was getting back her ancestral appetite, the taste of primary minerals, the unbridled satisfaction of what was the original food. She would put handfuls of earth in her pockets, and ate them in small bits without being seen, with a confused feeling of pleasure and rage, as she instructed her girl friends in the most difficult needlepoint and spoke about other men, who did not deserve the sacrifice of having one eat the whitewash on the walls because of them. The handfuls of earth made the only man who deserved that show of degradation less remote and more certain, as if the ground that he walked on with his fine patent leather boots in another part of the world were transmitting to her the weight and the temperature of his blood in a mineral savor that left a harsh after-taste in her mouth and a sediment of peace in her heart.

Translated by Gregory Rabassa

DEPRIVATION, STRANGE TASTES

Meat

VIRGILIO PIÑERA

IT HAPPENED SIMPLY, without pretense. For reasons that need not be explained, the town was suffering from a meat shortage. Everyone was alarmed, and rather bitter comments were heard; revenge was even spoken of. But, as always, the protests did not develop beyond threats, and soon the afflicted townspeople were devouring the most diverse vegetables.

Only Mr. Ansaldo didn't follow the order of the day. With great tranquility, he began to sharpen an enormous kitchen knife and then, dropping his pants to his knees, he cut a beautiful fillet from his left buttock. Having cleaned and dressed the fillet with salt and vinegar, he passed it through the broiler and finally fried it in the big pan he used on Sundays for making tortillas. He sat at the table and began to savor his beautiful fillet. Just then, there was a knock at the door: it was Ansaldo's neighbor coming to vent his frustrations.... Ansaldo, with an elegant gesture, showed his neighbor the beautiful fillet. When his neighbor asked about it, Ansaldo simply displayed his left buttock. The facts were laid bare. The neighbor, overwhelmed and moved, left without saying a word to return shortly with the mayor of the town. The latter expressed to Ansaldo his intense desire that his beloved townspeople be nourished—as was Ansaldo—by drawing on their private reserves, that is to say, each from their own meat. The issue was soon resolved, and after outbursts from the well educated, Ansaldo went to the main square of the town to offer—as he characteristically phrased it—"a practical demonstration for the masses."

Once there, he explained that each person could cut two fillets, from their left buttock, just like the flesh-colored plaster model he had hanging from a shining meathook. He showed how to cut two fillets not one, for if he had cut one beautiful fillet from his own left buttock, it was only right that no one should consume one fillet fewer. Once these points were cleared up, each person began to slice two fillets from his left buttock. It was a glorious spectacle, but it is requested that descriptions not be given out. Calculations were made concerning how long the town would enjoy the benefits of this meat. One distinguished physician predicted that a person weighing one hundred pounds (discounting viscera and the rest of the inedible organs) could eat meat for one hundred and forty days at the rate of half a pound a day. This calculation was, of course, deceptive. And what mattered was that each person could eat his beautiful fillet. Soon women were heard speaking of the advantages of Mr. Ansaldo's idea. For example, those who had devoured their breasts didn't need to cover their torsos with cloth, and their dresses reached just above the navel. Some women—though not all of them—no longer spoke at all, for they had gobbled up their tongues (which, by the way, is the delicacy of monarchs). In the streets, the most amusing scenes occurred: two

René Magritte, *Portrait* (1935)

DEPRIVATION, STRANGE TASTES

women who had not seen each other for a long time were unable to kiss each other: they had both used their lips to cook up some very successful fritters. The prison warden could not sign a convict's death sentence because he had eaten the fleshy tips of his fingers, which, according to the best "gourmets" (of which the warden was one), gave rise to the well-worn phrase "fingerlicking good."

There was some minor resistance. The ladies garment workers union registered their most formal protest with the appropriate authority, who responded by saying that it wasn't possible to create a slogan that might encourage women to patronize their tailors again. But the resistance was never significant, and did not in any way interrupt the townspeople's consumption of their own meat.

One of the most colorful events of that pleasant episode was the dissection of the town ballet dancer's last morsel of flesh. Out of respect for his art, he had left his beautiful toes for last. His neighbors observed that he had been extremely restless for days. There now remained only the fleshy tip of one big toe. At that point he invited his friends to attend the operation. In the middle of a bloody silence, he cut off the last portion, and, without even warming it up, dropped it into the hole that had once been his beautiful mouth. Everyone present suddenly became very serious.

But life went on, and that was the important thing. And if, by chance…? Was it because of this that the dancer's shoes could now be found in one of the rooms of the Museum of Illustrious Memorabilia? It's only certain that one of the most obese men in town (weighing over four hundred pounds) used up his whole reserve of disposable meat in the brief space of fifteen days (he was extremely fond of snacks and sweetmeats, and besides, his metabolism required large quantities). After a while, no one could ever find him. Evidently, he was hiding…. But he was not the only one to hide; in fact, many others began to adopt identical behavior. And so, one morning Mrs. Orfila got no answer when she asked her son (who was in the process of devouring his left earlobe) where he had put something. Neither pleas nor threats did any good. The expert in missing persons was called in, but he couldn't produce anything more than a small pile of excrement on the spot where Mrs. Orfila swore her beloved son had just been sitting at the moment she was questioning him. But these little disturbances did not undermine the happiness of the inhabitants in the least. For how could a town that was assured of its subsistence complain? Hadn't the crisis of public order caused by the meat shortage been definitively resolved? That the population was increasingly dropping out of sight was but a postscript to the fundamental issue and did not affect the people's determination to obtain their vital sustenance. Was that postscript the price that the flesh exacted from each? But it would be petty to ask any more such inopportune questions, now that this thoughtful community was perfectly well fed.

Translated by Mark Shafer

The Dead Eat

MILORAD PAVIĆ

"'CAIUS VERONIUS AET…Sextus Clodius Cai filius, Publilia tribu…Sorto Servilio… Veturia Aeia…'

"'Don't summon the dead!' Kalina warned him. 'Don't summon them—they'll come!'

"As soon as the sun had departed from the theater she removed the mushrooms and blood sausages from the fire and they began to eat. The acoustics were perfection itself, and each bite they took carried singly and with equal clarity to every seat, from the first to the eighth row, but everywhere in a different way, echoing the sound back to them at center stage. It was as if the spectators whose names had been carved into the fronts of the stone seats were eating together with the couple, or at least were greedily smacking their lips with every bite. One hundred and twenty pairs of dead ears were eavesdropping at pricked attention, and the entire theater was chewing along with the married couple, hungrily sniffing the aroma of the blood sausages. When they stopped eating, the dead stopped too, as if a morsel had got stuck in their throat, and they waited tensely to see what the young man and woman would do next. At such moments, Petkutin was especially careful not to cut his finger while slicing the food, because he had the feeling that the smell of human blood might throw the spectators off balance and that, as quick as a shooting pain, they might attack him and Kalina from the gallery and tear them apart, driven by their two-thousand-year-old thirst. He felt himself shudder, drew Kalina toward him, and kissed her. She kissed him, and they could hear the sound of 120 mouths kissing, as though those in the gallery were kissing too.

"After the meal, Petkutin threw the remainder of the blood sausages into the fire to burn and then doused the flames with wine; the sizzling of the dying fire in the theater was accompanied by a muffled 'Pssssss!' He was just about to return the knife to its case when the wind blew unexpectedly, depositing pollen on the stage. Petkutin sneezed and cut his hand. Blood spilled onto the warm stone and began to smell….

"At that moment 120 shrieking and howling dead souls descended upon them. Petkutin drew his sword, but they pulled Kalina apart, tearing her live flesh piece by piece until her cries became one with those emitted by the dead, and until she herself joined in devouring the still-uneaten parts of her own body.

"Petkutin did not know how many days had passed before he realized where the theater's exit was. He wandered about the stage around the dead fire and the remains of dinner until something invisible picked up his mantle from the ground and threw it over its shoulders. The empty cape came up to him and addressed him in Kalina's voice.

"Frightened, he embraced her, but beneath the fur and in the depths of her voice he could see nothing but the purple lining of the mantle.

"'Tell me,' Petkutin said to Kalina, clasping her in her arms, 'I feel as if some terrible thing happened to me here a thousand years ago. Someone was torn apart and devoured, and his blood still lies on the ground. I don't know if or when it really happened. Whom did they eat? You or me?'

"'Nothing happened to you; they didn't tear you apart,' replied Kalina. 'And it happened just a while ago, not a thousand years ago.'

"'But I do not see you. Which of the two of us is dead?'

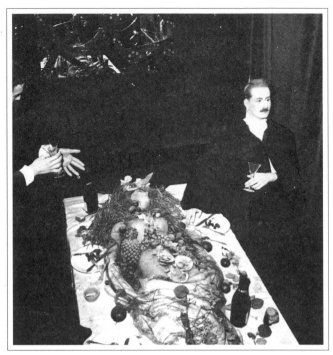

Meret Oppenheim, *Cannibal feast* (1959)

"'You do not see me, young man, because the living cannot see the dead. You can only hear my voice. As for me, I do not know who you are and cannot know until I have tasted a drop of your blood. But calm down—I do see you, I see you very well. And I know that you are alive.'

"'But, Kalina!' he cried. 'It's me, your Petkutin. Don't you recognize me? Just a moment ago, if it was a moment ago, you kissed me.'

"'What is the difference between a moment ago and a thousand years ago when things are the way they are now?'

"At those words Petkutin withdrew the knife, raised his finger to the spot where he imagined the invisible lips of his wife to be, and cut himself:

"The drop of blood released its smell but did not spill onto the stone, for Kalina eagerly awaited it on her lips. Once she recognized Petkutin, she screamed and tore him apart like carrion, greedily drank his blood, and tossed his bones into the theater, whence came the others in a swarm."

Translated by Christina Pribićević-Zorić

Breakfast

Wladimir Schohin, *Still Life* (ca. 1907)

Tea & Raspberry Preserves

ANDREY BIELY

ALEXANDER IVANOVICH opened his weary eyes: the night had been an event of gigantic proportions.

The transitional state between dream and waking felt like a jump from a fifth-story window. His senses had opened a breach, and into this breach he had plunged.

Waking had quickly precipitated him from there: his entire body ached. He was conscious of shivering violently. He had tossed all night long; something, certainly, must have happened...

The delirious flight continued along misty prospects, up and down the rungs of a strange ladder. Actually, he was suffering from a fever, which was raging through his body. Memory struggled to be heard, but eluded him; he tried vainly to connect things. Frightened—he had always feared sickness in solitude—he was determined to see it through.

"I must have quinine.... Yes, and strong tea...with raspberry preserves..."

He sighed involuntarily.

"I should abstain.... Perhaps I should not read *The Apocalypse*...maybe I should not look in on the house porter... nor chat with Stepka..."

Thinking of tea, Stepka, and *The Apocalypse* comforted him.

After washing his face in cold water from the faucet, he again felt the surge of the irrational. He glanced around his twenty-ruble garret room, a squalid place. His bed was made of cracked boards placed across wooden trestles, showing the stains of dried bedbugs. The boards were covered with a very hard mattress; the red and blue stripes were faded from the woven bedcover; traces of them had been removed not by dirt but by many years of hard use.

A small ikon depicting the prayer of Seraphim Sarovsky hung in a corner: under his shirt Alexander Ivanovich wore a cross.

In addition to the bed, the room contained a small planed table, such as is commonly used for holding wash basins and is usually sold in country markets. It served both as a writing table and night table; there was no wash basin.

Alexander Ivanovich used a spigot and a sardine tin for his piece of Kazan soap. There was also a clothes rack, under which showed the tip of a worn slipper. In a dream he had once seen a slipper behaving as if it were alive like a dog or a cat; it had shuffled along autonomously, crawling about in the corners with a rustling noise; when he had offered to feed it some soft musty bread, the shuffling creature had bitten his finger; he had awakened. A bulging tan suitcase, which had lost its original form, was also in the room.

All the decorations of the room were overshadowed by the color of the very ugly and somber wallpaper: dark yellow, darkish brown with damp stains. At night wood-lice crawled over it.

Alexander Ivanovich Doodkin surveyed his habitation; he longed to be outdoors, in the unclean fog, rubbing shoulders, mingling with other backs and greenish faces, on a Petersburg prospect.

Layers of October fog clung to the windowpane; he felt a desire to be overwhelmed by the fog, to drown in it the nonsense which irritated his brain, to extinguish the surges of delirium by exercising his legs. He wanted to stride from prospect to prospect, from street to street, until his brain was numbed, and then collapse at a tavern table and burn out his organs with vodka.

He put on his thin overcoat and thought, "I really ought to take some quinine! But what's the good of quinine?

"I'd better have some strong tea with raspberry preserves!…"

Translated by John Cournos

Coffee, Rolls, and Honey

CARL VAN VECHTEN

Edward Weston, *Hot Coffee, Mojave Desert* (1937)

IN THE MORNINGS, Peter and I breakfasted together in the garden, whither was borne us by the cynical butler a tray with individual coffee percolators, a plate of fresh rolls, and a bowl of honey. The peacocks strutted the terrace and the breeze blew the branches of the fragrant gardenias across our noses. In the distance, the bells of Florence softly tolled.

peanuts discover each other as butter

CHARLEY GEORGE

peanut **PEANUT** peanut peanut *peanut*
peanut peanut PEANUT PEANUT *peanut*
peanut peanut peanut **peanut** peanu
t *peanut* PEANUT peanut peanut **p**
eanut peanut *PEANUT* peanut
peanut peanut **PEANUT** *pean*
ut peanut peanut peanut p
anut PEANUT peanut *p*
anut peanut **peanut**
peanut peanut PE
ANUT peanut
peanut PEA
NUT pe
pean
u
t   t
p   p*t*

peap*ea*rtnutpea*p*tu*t*nut*nut*n*ut*n*peaut*pea   p tp
*n*upe*pe*nutppea*tt*t*t*nu*t*nu*pepenua*nutpetat   t *p*t*p
pntnpntpp*nnp*ntttppnnpntntntnpptnnpnn   tppt t   t *p*   p p   t pt p t p
euueauueeuueaueeuuueeaeueuueeeaea   nn nn   nnn   t t *t*   p
         eu   nnn   p *p* p
         eu   nnn   p *t*tp
         eu   nnn   t
         eu
         eu   nnn
         eu
         eu   nnn   nnnnnn   nnnn
         eueueu   eueueu   eueueu   eueueu   eueu
         eueueu   eueueu   eueueu   eueueu   eueu
         eueueu   eueueu   eueueu   eueueu   eueu
         eueueu   eueueu   eueueu   eueueu   eueu
         eueueu   eueueu   eueueu   eueueu   eueu

Savory Oatmeal Breakfast

from Nanao Sokaki

ALLEN GINSBERG

For two portions:

1 cup oatmeal in 2 cups boiling water.
Add: 5 Chopped Fresh Mushrooms
    any leftover meat or fish sliced or cubed
    Some chopped onion, pepper, and/or peas—
    A handful of fresh celery, spinach, etc.
*   2 big cloves garlic chopped, or 3 or 5.
*   1 chunk chopped fresh ginger—half a pinky-tip size chunk.

— • —

    hacking leftover meat, add
    small palm-full of pre-soaked dried seaweed
    2 or 3 sliced pre-soaked dried black
        Japanese mushrooms [pre-soak = 5 minutes]
    Small palm-full of dried squid strings.
*   Sprinkling of dried Bonito flakes.

any combination of these or similar elements.

    *[Garlic, Ginger, Bonito Flakes, basic, though.]

Meat or especially squid should be put in at beginning
    with oatmeal. Unless it's rare beef. The rest later.
Can sprinkle with brown or roast sesame seeds
    and chopped chives or spring onions, fine chop'd,
    or "prepared seaweed" condiment.
Can serve with raw egg on top. & Soy Sauce.
    or a little "Sechuan hot bean paste with dried squid."

Katz Curried Oatmeal

STEVE KATZ

I NEVER EXPECTED to express this as a recipe. I like to think of it as the culmination of a morning mode, following the processes of eyelid lifts and other sophisticated exercises that result in eventual verticality. One happy result of following these instructions with some sincerity is that you will find yourself vertical by a seascape so beautiful I wouldn't trust a description of it to the world's best writers. That's the shores of Cape Breton, preferably at dawn—erect at dawn, supine by sunset. You go there to get the oatmeal, *Ogilvie's Scotch Style Oatmeal,* generally for sale at the Co-op in Inverness or at McLellans. You can probably get it at other stores elsewhere in Nova Scotia and Canada, but I can't see why you would want to. If you can't go that far, and want to simulate the recipe, I suggest you avoid Quaker Oats and find some loose steel-cut oats in a health food or bulk grain outlet. Quaker Oats don't give you the nutty texture you want for the awakening this dish ideally provides.

To cook *1 cup* of these oats you will need *4 to 5 cups of freshly drawn spring water.* This water is best from the hills of Foot Cape, but I am sure you can find an adequate substitute. Many people like to cook the oats in a double-boiler on a low heat throughout the night. I have tried that and it made for some soft oats, but I prefer the texture you get cooking them directly over the flame, and stirring frequently. Bring the water to a rolling boil, add the oats, lower the heat to a simmer, and stir frequently. The oats foam up and threaten to escape the pot at first, but you will find that as you tend them, they will calm down and become quite tame to your attention.

These oats take twenty minutes to a half hour to reach their optimum texture, which for me is more or less "al dente." When they are about half way you can add the spices. If you have a preferred *curry powder* you can stir in *½ to a full teaspoon* of that, according to taste. I've liked some curry powders, but what I have consistently used and preferred is the following combination of *⅛ teaspoon each of cumin, ground coriander, turmeric, and cayenne.* The amounts of each can vary according to taste. Add salt also to taste. At least five minutes before the oats are ready add ½ cup of diced dried fruit. I enjoy a combination of raisins, black or golden, preferably not treated with sugar, and unsulphured dried apricots. After you add the fruit check occasionally to see how much water it absorbs, and if the pot needs it, add some boiling water.

To finish the porridge sauté some *raw sunflower seeds* in butter. I prefer the lightly salted butter of Tatamagouche, when I can get it. When the sunnies are light brown pour them into the nicely bubbling porridge. You will hear a heavenly hiss from the disturbance of steam that for the moment will drown out the sound of the waves breaking.

Four to six of your friends are sitting outside the tipi, or on the deck, or with their feet dangling off the bank, as they watch the early sunlight come over the hill to touch the crests of the waves. This should fill a nice bowl for each of them, that will warm their bellies for much of the day. Serve it to them with a bowl of *yogurt*, and some coffee brewed with cardomon. They are your friends, and there will never be another morning like this morning.

    1 cup oats (Ogilvie's Scotch Style, or steel cut)

    4 – 5 cups spring water

    ½ – 1 tsp curry or ⅛ tsp each cumin, ground coriander, turmeric,
            cayenne

    salt

    ½ cup diced dried fruit

    ½ cup sunflower seeds

    yogurt

    butter

    yogurt

Roubaud's Law of Butter Croissants

JACQUES ROUBAUD

CONTRARY TO any conclusions that might be drawn from my extremely *perfective* (in the Russian verb sense) description, a breakfast of cookies (which could just as well be crumbly Chinese wafers, or simple Clément melba toast smothered in jam (on special occasions, after a trip to the Alésia supermarket, for a few mornings, Scottish shortbread (of (Celtic) inspiration akin to the *Traou-Mad,* but with a more compact shape and consistency (a difference in which I sense some Pict influence, even more palpable no doubt in the *baps,* manifestations of Pictitude-in-itself, dear to Saki's aunt, and which I've never yet tasted)))) and instant coffee was a recent practice, necessitated by my procedures for getting the prose under way and its schedule demands, which in the past, as today, were strange. On moving to Rue de la Harpe, almost one year before (at the beginning of 1979), at first I looked in the vicinity for friendly café where in

the mornings, an hour or two after getting up, I could have a *grand crème* with two *beurres* (or *two croissants*) and read an English novel, following my already long-established custom. I quickly had to give up the idea.

For even more so than in the neighborhood around Place Clichy from which I was moving, the ever-later opening hours of cafés would have compelled me to push back my own waking time until almost eight o'clock (which is impossible) or to wait, which I don't like to do. Thus I had resigned myself to buying croissants from the bakery (by way of compensatory reparations, unilaterally deciding to switch from plain to butter croissants). I would reach this bakery, located on Boulevard Saint-Germain, by walking along Rue de la Parcheminerie, followed by Rue Boutebrie. The ideal *croissant* (and this has to do, naturally, with the Parisian croissant, since in whatever town I've tried them provincial croissants have been disasters), the croissant that might be labeled the *archetypal butter croissant,*

offers the following features: a very elongated diamond, rounded at the tips but with an almost straight body (only the *plain croissant,* and it alone, has a lunar, ottomanlike look)—golden—plump—not too well done—nor too white or starchy—staining your fingers through the India paper that wraps, or rather holds it together—still warm (from the oven it has recently left, it has not yet cooled) (after reheating—which works well perhaps with "quiches" or poultry, and with those loathsome discoids the French dub "pizzas"—croissants turn crunchy, which is horrible, and rancid, because of the butter).

It has three principal components, and three interlocking meaty compartments protected by a tender shell that lends it certain similarities to a young lobster. The center section is, in this croissant-lobster homomorphism, the body of the crustacean; the end parts are the pincerless claws. It's an extremely stylized lobster, a *formal lobster,* in short. For the croissant to be perfect, a simple tug on each "claw" should easily pull them apart from the "body," each trailing along an oblique, tapering excrescence of inner meat, subtracted from the center, extracted, as it were, effortlessly from the still very warm innards of the croissant, without making crumbs, or any sound, or rips. I openly lay claim to the discovery of this correspondence, this structural morphism (at least I have found no "plagiarism by anticipation") which I propose calling *Roubaud's Law of Butter Croissants.*

It is, of course, impossible nowadays to find a definitive croissant composed in accordance with this axiom and fulfilling my dream. Perhaps the ideal croissant only ever existed as a best-case scenario, a formal essence that could only find its remote approximation in actually existing croissants. Those from the boulevard bakery, even though the best in the neighborhood, only modestly approximated this ideal. Still, I was delighted to have found them, so greatly did the general worthlessness of modern croissants make me shudder. Now, there are bakeries (I could name names!) where you are underhandedly sold day-old croissants (nevertheless set aside tacitly and traditionally for third-class hotels and the most mediocre and stingy cafés). They are lusterless, misshapen, shopworn, smelly, with the look of stale ocean fish at the stall of a Jurassic fishmonger, around August 15th, before freezers were invented. There are croissants at once puny and charred; others with no discernible shape, still raw; yet others—an especially unpleasant cat-

Salvador Dali, *Basket of Bread* (1926)

egory—whose crust has been slightly carmelized with extra sugar to tart them up (most treacherous, these, for you can't spy them with a cursory glance, and then have to spit them out after the first bite); others still, whose disgraceful tips stick up like jutting chins. And that's not all! More often than not, it takes me just a tenth of a second to judge a bakery by scrutinizing its croissant shelves, and I am truthbound to swear that Paris, from this point of view, is increasingly being transformed into a chamber of horrors (paralleling the decadence, which I fear irremediable, of the baguette).

My bakery during that period (like the Tranchant Bakery before it, on Rue de Clichy) seemed to be a vestige of a former time; it also maintained the age-old tradition of having a croissant waitress who was a blonde, milk-white dairy damsel (of the "fat lazy blonde" variety), soft, bovine, listless, whose flesh appeared to be plumped by a partial, hasty, and clandestine ingestion of an enormous quantity of croissants surreptitiously filched at the oven door. Her face came to life only to indicate her gratitude from the first second she identified me as a soul mate, a fellow croissant lover; she was even so intellectually stimulated that one day she answered my invariable order of "Two butter croissants, not too well done, please" with a "Four croissants this morning?"; and the still unset crust of her face trembled an instant before falling flat in the mold. But despite my silent exhortations, she never attained the double antonymic variation: "Four croissants, well done?"

Hot croissants in hand, wrapped in their paper, I sped home, for they must still be warm to the bite at the requisite time. There is an optimum moment for consuming croissants, a "Machiavellian moment" (in the Pocockian sense); a ritual of gestures, accompanied by an inward preparation.

Furthermore, among the group of croissant eaters (croissants in general, plain as well as butter) there are two contending schools: the dry school and the wet school. This means: after having prepared a bowl of café au lait (I still hadn't given up milk), hot but not scalding, I dipped the croissant wing (the leg rather) (let's preserve a metaphoric consistency) that I pulled off (let's imagine a perfect croissant, satisfying Roubaud's Law for the sake of the description) in such fashion that it becomes moist, saturated, softens, but without dissolving, *without coming undone.* I proceeded likewise with the other leg; then with the center part of the thus dismembered body (starting with the *left* leg!). If the croissant were perfect (herein lies an indisputable test of its degree of perfection) (along Roubaud's Croissant scale), provided that the correct procedures have been carried out, at the bottom of the bowl there should remain no trace of its disappearance. *A true croissant never crumbles.* A croissant so moist that it collapses into a variation of a rain-sodden cardboard box in some empty lot on the city outskirts makes me recoil as much as the opposite sort, croissants so dry that they hurt my mouth on contact. Just as a thin sprinkle of rain on a summer evening at the seashore in the intense heat, dampening the dust at an outdoor café, settling the dryness, releasing the sudden fragrance of earth, flowers, shadow and plane trees, gives you a pang of nostalgia, so the perfect caffeinated moistness lending the perfect aroma, the perfect consistency to the croissant, makes you believe, if only for one precarious moment, in the possibility of a good day ahead. By giving up croissants, I had, as is plain to see, made a serious sacrifice for my prose; but I expected no reward in return.

Orange Julius

BARBARA GUEST

IN LOS ANGELES when I was a child there was a modest food shop that opened onto the sidewalk. This sacred place was on the corner of Hope Street at an angle from Pershing Square. It was also across the street from a movie palace where live dance shows played in the intermission—now the landmark Academy Theatre. The theatre was the scene of my devotions, but the food and drink shop shared with it a culinary promise. As at Delphi before entering the temple of Apollo I refreshed myself at this Parnassian Spring. The *Original* Orange Julius was served here. Make no mistake about that as its copy was later served all over town.

No homemade Orange Julius could compete with that made on Hope Street with what was sworn to be real cream, and real oranges. It may have been the froth that lathered the glass as the fresh orange liquid fell from the spigot while I stood beside the lively, dedicated counter. What I remember is that this drink ennobled the Los Angeles of my youth with its evocation of golden groves sheltered by the tall and fragrant eucalyptus that one entered as soon as the portals of far-off Whittier were passed.

This is the recipe for the drink as we served it at home.

ORANGE JULIUS

⅔'s glass of freshly squeezed orange juice
add 1 well beaten egg
fill glass to top with light cream (or milk, not skim)
stir or use blender
serves one person

Who was Julius? The proprietor? I never asked. To me he was imperial.

Breakfast

THOMAS WOLFE

IN THE MORNING they rose in a house pungent with breakfast cookery, and they sat at a smoking table loaded with brains and eggs, ham, hot biscuit, fried apples seething in their gummed syrups, honey, golden butter, fried steak, scalding coffee. Or there were stacked batter-cakes, rum-colored molasses, fragrant brown sausages, a bowl of wet cherries, plums, fat juicy bacon, jam.

Douglas Messerli, *Eggs* (1978)

The Inner Organs of Beasts & Fowls

JAMES JOYCE

MR LEOPOLD BLOOM ate with rel-
ish the inner organs of beasts and fowls.
He liked thick giblet soup, nutty giz-
zards, a stuffed roast heart, liver slices
fried with crustcrumbs, fried hencod's
roes. Most of all he liked grilled mutton
kidneys which gave to his palate a fine
tang of faintly scented urine.

Kidneys were in his mind as he moved
about the kitchen softly, righting her
breakfast things on the humpy tray. Gelid
light and air were in the kitchen but out
of doors gentle summer morning everywhere. Made him feel a bit peckish.

The coals were reddening.

Another slice of bread and butter: three, four: right. She didn't like her plate full. Right. He turned from the tray, lifted the kettle off the hob and set it sideways on the fire. It sat there, dull and squat, its spout stuck out. Cup of tea soon. Good. Mouth dry. The cat walked stiffly round a leg of the table with tail on high.

—Mkgnao!

—O, there you are, Mr Bloom said, turning from the fire.

The cat mewed in answer and stalked again stiffly round a leg of the table, mewing. Just how she stalks over my writingtable. Prr. Scratch my head. Prr.

Mr Bloom watched curiously, kindly, the lithe black form. Clean to see: the gloss of her sleek hide, the white button under the butt of her tail, the green flashing eyes. He bent down to her, his hands on his knees.

—Milk for the pussens, he said.

—Mrkgnao! the cat cried.

They call them stupid. They understand what we say better than we understand them. She understands all she wants to. Vindictive too. Wonder what I look like to her. Height of a tower? No, she can jump me.

—Afraid of the chickens she is, he said mockingly. Afraid of the chookchooks. I never saw such a stupid pussens as the pussens.

Cruel. Her nature. Curious mice never squeal. Seem to like it.

—Mrkrgnao! the cat said loudly.

She blinked up out of her avid shameclosing eyes, mewing plaintively and long, showing him her milkwhite teeth. He watched the dark eyeslits narrowing with greed till her eyes were green stones. Then he went to the dresser, took the jug Hanlon's milkman had just filled for him, poured warmbubbled milk on a saucer and set it slowly on the floor.

—Gurrhr! she cried, running to lap.

He watched the bristles shining wirily in the weak light as she tipped three times and licked lightly. Wonder is it true if you clip them they can't mouse after. Why? They shine in the dark, perhaps, the tips. Or kind of feelers in the dark, perhaps.

He listened to her licking lap. Ham and eggs, no. No good eggs with this drouth. Want pure fresh water. Thursday: not a good day either for a mutton kidney at Buckley's. Fried with butter, a shake of pepper. Better a pork kidney at Dlugacz's. While the kettle is boiling. She lapped slower, then licking the saucer clean. Why are their tongues so rough? To lap better, all porous holes. Nothing she can eat? He glanced round him. No.

On quietly creaky boots he went up the staircase to the hall, paused by the bedroom door. She might like something tasty. Thin bread and butter she likes in the morning. Still perhaps: once in a way.

He said softly in the bare hall:

—I am going round the corner. Be back in a minute.

And when he had heard his voice say it he added:

—You don't want anything for breakfast?

A sleepy soft grunt answered:

—Mn.

Haymaker's Breakfast

AUGUST STRINDBERG

BY EIGHT IN THE MORNING the meadow near the spring had the appearance of newly drilled arable land. It was flat as a hand, and the hay lay in long swaths. Now the haymakers looked over their handiwork and examined the workmanship; and Rundquist found himself singled out for incompetence by those chosen as judges. Wherever he had advanced with his scythe, you could see ring after ring of tufts and patches of grass that he had left standing. Rundquist defended himself by saying that he just couldn't take his eyes off the girl who had been assigned to him— after all, it was not every day that he had a girl at his heels.

At this moment, Clara let out an *ahoy,* calling the haymakers to breakfast up on the hill. The brandy bottle glimmered in the sun, and the keg of near-beer was opened; the potatoes steamed in the caldron on the hearthstone, and the herrings clouded the plates with moisture; butter had been placed on the table, the bread had been cut, the brandy had been passed, and the meal was underway.

Translated by Arvid Paulson

Grant Wood, *Dinner for Threshers* (1933)

Spices, Soups, Sauces, Light Meals, Lunches

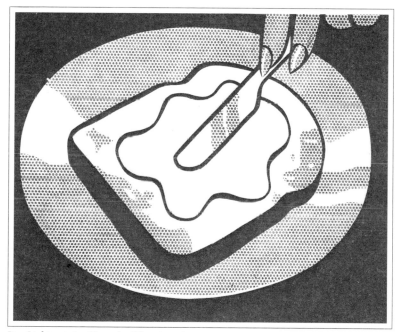

Roy Lichtenstein, *Mustard on White* (1963)

⊗

Salt

MALCOLM DE CHAZAL

SPICES WOUND our sense of taste; salt dresses the wound. Spices without salt make the mouth salivate after the feast is over like a wound that wells up with blood.

Salt fills up the cracks in food. When a dish lacks salt our sense of taste has to feel its way along carefully in order not to stumble.

Salt gives the taste buds a donkey ride.

Salt is the police of taste. As the police protect the weak against the strong, salt keeps each of the various flavors of a course in place as much as possible and prevents them from unequal struggle, restraining the stronger from dominating the weaker. As in a well-directed orchestra the brasses often drown out the violins without "destroying" them, and the violins similarly overpower the basses; so in food salt will prevent the vinegar from ruining the taste of the onions, red peppers from overcoming green pepper, and mustard from relegating ginger to the back of the palate.

Nothing in the realm of taste combines tasting and smelling as well as vinegar. One whiff of vinegar in the salad wafts the whole concoction into your mouth. Your neighbor's tart armpits assailing your nostrils at table puts an edge on your food.

The Good Soup

FRIEDRICH ACHLEITNER

1

this is frau kreil. she has a beautiful tray in her large hands. she is going to throw the beautiful tray on the blue table. what is on the beautiful tray. yellow glasses. long forks. sharp knives. all these are necessary things. here are two more sharp knives. sticky spoons. moist plates. sticky spoons and moist plates are necessary things. frau kreil takes a long fork and a sharp knife from the beautiful tray. she throws them on the blue table. the moist plates follow. soon all necessary things will be on the blue table.

2

frau kreil makes good soup. she is going to make good soup from white milk and young potatoes. this is white milk. frau kreil makes good soup. she is going to make good soup from white cow milk and young potatoes. this is a black cow. black cows are useful animals. here are some more useful animals. the round pig. the woolly sheep. the noble horse. black cows give white milk. frau kreil throws the white milk from the glass bottle into the shallow cup. the red apple lies on the cool ground. the young potato lies in the cool ground. young potatoes are green plants. this is a green plant. these are small roots. this is a long fork. we take the young potatoes out of the cool ground with a long fork.

3

thick stream. a merry flame. the violet pot is on the merry flame. the merry flame is under the violet pot. thick steam comes out of the glass bottle. in the glass bottle is brown water; it is very warm. the merry flame is under the glass bottle. this is purple ice. the purple ice is in the brown water. purple ice is cold. purple ice is cold and hard. and this is a medium piece of purple ice. a slim thermometer. purple ice is cold. the merry flame is warm.

4

the golden kitchen clock hangs on the silver wall. the golden kitchen clock has two pointed hands. the long pointed hand is the pointed minute hand. the short minute is an exact time measurement. the medium pointed hand is the pointed hour hand. the exact hour is an exact time measurement. the slim thermometer. the slim thermometer has exact degrees. this is an exact degree. warm. cold. very cold. and this is an exact meter. an exact meter has one hundred centimeter. this is frau kreil's able foot. able feet. this is herr kreil's able foot. it is thirty exact centimeter long.

5

a cheerful bird. a healthy tree. the other two cheerful birds are not screaming in the healthy tree. they are in the dense air. a new airplane. these are more new airplanes. these new airplanes are not in the dense air. the broad face of the broad man. the dense air goes through his broad nose. it goes through his broad mouth into his broad body. the dense air comes back out of his broad body. it goes in. it comes out. this is the broad man's warm breath. now the dense air comes out of his broad mouth. it is cold.

6

the brown water in the violet pot is very warm. thick steam comes out of the violet pot. the dense air above the merry flame is very warm. it rises. the dense air underneath the merry flame is not very warm. it rises up to the merry flame. and this is a painted icebox. the dense air in the painted icebox is very cold. the glass bottle of white milk. these are fragile eggs. the tall door of the painted icebox is closed again. the white milk and the fragile eggs are in the painted icebox. the silver walls and the cold bottom of the painted icebox are thick. this is a thin line. this is a thick line. warm air. cold air. warm air. the warm air does not go into the painted icebox.

7

herr kreil is glad. this is bloody meat. this is sour bread. this is a piece of sour bread. this is low-fat cheese. we make low-fat cheese from white milk. soft butter. the soft butter is on the moist plate. we make soft butter from white milk. frau kreil keeps the soft butter and the white milk in the painted icebox. she also keeps the low-fat cheese there. red apples. sweet oranges. sweet pears. sweet plums. sweet cherries. sweet peaches. sweet raspberries. sweet strawberries. sweet gooseberries. sweet fruit. what time is it. it is five o'clock. frau kreil is going to make the good soup.

8

what time is it. it is half past five. frau kreil is making a soup. it is forty minutes past five. the young potatoes are in the violet pot. frau kreil has a long fork in her large hand. the young potatoes are hard. the long fork does not go through them. it is fifty minutes past five. the young potatoes are soft. the long fork goes through the young potatoes. frau kreil takes the young potatoes out of the violet pot and throws them on the moist plate. they were in the violet pot. they were hard. now they are soft. frau kreil put white milk and soft butter with the potatoes. now they are very soft.

9

herr kreil has a piece of low-fat cheese between his bandaged fingers. he throws the piece of low-fat cheese into his broad mouth. now he has the piece of low-fat cheese between his real teeth. the low-fat cheese is not soft. herr kreil's real teeth do not go through it. meanwhile frau kreil has thrown the young potatoes, the white milk and the other necessary things into the violet pot. coarse salt. the violet pot is over the merry flame. the light lid is on the violet pot. the merry flame is very small. the light lid goes clopity clop. this dark building is very large. however this dark building is also very small.

10

what time is it. it is six o'clock. frau kreil takes a sticky spoon of good soup in her broad mouth. the good soup is ready. it is good. now she throws the good soup into the moist plate. it was in the violet pot. now it is in the moist plates. frau kreil made the good soup. the good soup is ready. the good soup is good.

Translated by Rosmarie Waldrop

Poss

SAMUEL BECKETT

MR KNOTT'S MEALS gave very little trouble.

On Saturday night a sufficient quantity of food was prepared and cooked to carry Mr Knott through the week.

This dish contained foods of various kinds, such as soup of various kinds, fish, eggs, game, poultry, meat, cheese, fruit, all of various kinds, and of course bread and butter, and it contained also the more usual beverages, such as absinthe, mineral water, tea, coffee, milk, stout, beer, whiskey, brandy, wine and water, and it contained also many things to take for the good of the health, such as insulin, digitalin, calomel, iodine, laudanum, mercury, coal, iron, camomille and worm-powder, and of course salt and mustard, pepper and sugar, and of course a little salicylic acid, to delay fermentation.

All these things, and many others too numerous to mention, were well mixed together in the famous pot and boiled for four hours, until the consistence of a mess, or poss, was obtained, and all the good things to eat, and all the good things to drink, and all the good things to take for the good of the health were inextricably mingled and transformed into a single good thing that was neither food, nor drink, nor physic, but quite a new good thing, and of which the tiniest spoonful at once opened the appetite and closed it, excited and stilled the thirst, compromised and stimulated the body's vital functions, and went pleasantly to the head.

It fell to Watt to weigh, to measure and to count, with the utmost exactness, the ingredients that composed this dish, and to dress for the the pot those that required dressing, and to mix them thoroughly together without loss, so that not one could be distinguished from another, and to put them on to boil, and when boiling to keep them on the boil, and when boiled to take them off the boil and put out to cool, in a cool place. This was a task that taxed Watt's powers, both of mind and of body, to the utmost, it was so delicate, and rude. And in warm weather it sometimes happened, as he mixed, stripped to the waist, and plying with both hands the great iron rod, that tears would fall, tears of mental fatigue, from his face, into the pot, and from his chest, and out from under his arms, beads of moisture, provoked by his exertions, into the pot also. His moral reserves also were severely tried, so great was his sense of responsibility. For he knew, as though he had been told, that the receipt of this dish had never varied, since its establishment, long long before, and that the choice, the dosage and the quantities of the elements employed had been calculated, with the most minute exactness, to afford Mr Knott, in a course of fourteen full meals, that is to say, seven full luncheons, and seven full dinners, the maximum of pleasure compatible with the protraction of his health.

This dish was served to Mr Knott, cold, in a bowl, at twelve o'clock noon sharp and at seven P.M. exactly, all the year round.

That is to say that Watt carried in the bowl, full, to the dining-room at those hours, and left it on the table. An hour later he went back and took it away, in whatever state Mr Knott had left it. If the bowl still contained food, then Watt transferred this food to the dog's dish. But if it was empty, then Watt washed it up, in readiness for the next meal.

Andy Warhol, *4 Campbell's Soup Cans* (1962)

Bowl of Progresso Minestrone

WILLIAM CORBETT

thin broth, mushy vegetables
          but hot
as everywhichway wind
scatters predicted rain
and hailstones (we'll see)
big as hailstones
even this tasteless bowl
recalls Florentine winter lunches:
bread soup,
clear broth with tiny
ricelike pasta,
risotto con funghi,
con gorgonzola,
dip sliced fennel,
young artichoke petals
in salty green olive oil,
glass after glass
red Tuscan summer wine . . .
Clouds drift, the Arno slithers
snakegreen but not too shallow
for longpoled fishermen,
trunks of tackle,
decked out in crisp fishing regalia.
Remember boys kicking their

ball shouts of "Dai, dai!"
foggy midnight before the Innocenti;
remember footfalls on stone slabs,
conversations and laughter rising
up the dark narrow streets
noises up a stone chimney;
remember you stared so hard
the man laughed
and pushed over his plate of sausage;
remember green oranges
in a frosty courtyard,
dead pigeons at the doors
of Santa Maria Novella;
remember Pensione Rigatti
Marni and Gabrielle announce their wedding
but it was not to be
and will never be.
          Who can blame error?
White clouds depart
wind picks up,
off the roof pinecones clatter
clouds of fog and spray
and out of the west, cold.
Enough sadness to go round

this green world
now rain comes down
the dinner hour in Florence
Marni in Amsterdam.

Marcel Broodthaer's *La Soupe de Daguerre* (1976)

Corn Soup & Fry Bread

DIANE & JEROME ROTHENBERG

For several years before 1972 to 1974, we lived on the Allegany Seneca Reservation in Salamanca, New York. Food was among the first things we exchanged—poetry only later and never really fully. From our end the items served were dishes such as sukiyaki or pumpernickel rye; from theirs the common foods of rural America and two specially prepared dishes that indicated that a uniquely Native American festivity was underway. One of those dishes was "corn soup" (more specifically "hulled corn soup" [hominy], because there are other ways of using corn in soups), and the other one was "fry bread." During the years that we lived in Salamanca, we encountered both of these dishes many times and in variant versions. Different people whom we knew approached their preparation in individualized ways—congruent always with their own tastes, their interest in food preparation, and their concern (or lack of it) with "authenticity." When we reproduce those dishes now for special occasions of our own, these same considerations inform our sense of how to go about

it. As a reflection on the issue of "authenticity" in the preparation of traditional foods— as well as the contribution of a couple of good recipes to the present volume—we offer up the following.

"AUTHENTIC" HULLED CORN SOUP à la Archie Johnson, who knows how to do many things the "old way."

    1 quart dry corn
    1 pint clean hardwood ashes
    Water to cover

Place in cast iron kettle, and bring to a boil. Boil until the hulls slip off the kernels (about 20 minutes). Place in corn basket, and rinse in cold water until clean. Reboil corn in water until suds form, and rinse again in basket. Repeat once more.

    ¾ lb. salt pork cut up
    ¼ lb. dried red kidney beans (presoaked)
    Prepared corn (hominy) from first step

Boil all together in kettle for 3 or 4 hours. Makes about 4 quarts of soup.

"CONVENIENT" HULLED CORN SOUP à la Richard Johnny John, who loves it but, for all kinds of reasons, takes short cuts.

    3 large cans of hominy (undrained)
    1 can of red beans (undrained)
    1 lb. pork (or maybe more if using spareribs)
Water enough to create a thick soup. Cook everything together until the pork is done.

"ROTHENBERG" HULLED CORN SOUP, being a variation of Dick Johnny John's recipe, but accommodating to non-Seneca expectations.

    2 lbs. of pork with bones
    1 carrot
    Couple of handfuls of celery and celery tops
    1 onion
    Parsley
    Salt and pepper to taste
    Water to cover

Cook until pork is separating from bones. Drain through a strainer, and save the pieces of meat.

3 large cans of hominy (undrained)

1 can of red beans (undrained)

Combine broth, pork, and canned ingredients, and cook together for a few minutes. Season to taste.

*

FRY BREAD is known among the Senecas as "Ghost Bread," because it is always included in the feast that follows the ten days of mourning after a death. A look at the ingredients suggests immediately that even the "authentic" version depends entirely on store bought ingredients; yet fry bread, with minor variations in shape and ingredients, is emblematically "Indian" all through North America.

2 cups white flour

3 tsp. baking powder

2 tblsp. sugar

Pinch salt

1 cup water

Knead together, and let stand for 15 minutes. Break off golf-ball sized pieces, and roll each out, using flour to prevent sticking. Stab with a fork twice through the center of each. Fry in deep fat until brown on both sides. Eat hot.

FRY BREAD à la Thelma Shane, one of the best cooks around.

Same as above but add along with other ingredients:

2 tblsp. oil

½ small can crushed pineapple.

Proceed as above. Roll out ½ inch thick, and fry until brown. (Thelma usually serves these with margarine and preserves, accompanied regularly by coffee.)

"FAST FRY BREAD," which is what you usually get at *our* feasts. This recipe was revealed to us at an Indian Foods Dinner—a tourist-oriented feast offered, as a fund-raiser, around Thanksgiving, i.e. harvest time. One or another Seneca organization is allowed to prepare the dinner each year, at which time they serve hundreds of diners, both white and Indian, who have reserved well in advance, eager for the opportunity to taste the variety and abundance of "authentic" Seneca food. The Senecas with whom we ate would snicker a little when fry bread was presented in the following way:

Open a tube of store-bought prepared biscuits (not the sourdough type, but it hardly matters). Separate the biscuits, and flatten each using a little flour to prevent sticking. Pierce with the tines of a fork, and fry in deep fat. They rise and brown very quickly, so keep watching. Drain and serve.

With a genuine taste for the inauthentic (as much as for its counterpart), we have made this recipe our own.

Food

ROBERT WALSER

VEAL FRICANDEAU is frightful stuff. Boeuf à la mode is horrid. Cheese eaten with tea is splendid. Some people like to eat fried potatoes with cheese. Macaroni? My favorite dish. But it has to be reeking with cheese, has to be absolutely dripping with cheese. Actually I'm fascinated by kitchens; I'd probably have made a good cook or chef. The poetry I'd have cooked up would have been far better, far tastier than what springs from the cold, pointy nib of my pen. I'd have been able to serve a duke to satisfaction.

Why my strong predilection for food? Watching people eat is a pleasure for me. How prettily, by the way, cats lap up milk. My cat always used to share my plate with me. With her black paw, she'd snatch the best morsels from beneath my very nose. I was helpless to stop her; I couldn't possibly have punished her for her naughtiness. Horses have such a charming way of eating. A great many humans don't eat nearly so nicely. My thoughts now lead me to genuine Kiel sprats. The first time I ate sprats, I thought I was in heaven. Nowadays they rate rather low in my book. Raw ham is always a healthy meal; cooked, it's too slippery. I've no craving for sweets, but love bread smeared or spread with butter, all by itself. But it has to be country bread. City bread is too superficially baked; it tends to lack character.

Entire meals can put me in raptures, particularly when they're served up with style. But it's heavenly to partake of a grilled herring in a simple pub. Sausages, for instance bockwurst, bierwurst, and wienerwurst, are too repellent and too likely to come up on you. They make one feel uncouth. One should avoid that sort of thing. On the other hand, you can pop some crisp roast beef into my mouth for me to gobble up any time you please; just make sure it's properly laced with bacon fat and swimming in sauce. From time to time boiled potatoes also receive my stamp of approval. Someone who knows how to cook a potato in such a way that it represents an enticing comestible in its own right proves he has a real flair for the culinary art, for this art, too, has its pinnacles, its laurel leaves, like any other.

Discussing the masterpieces and crown jewels of this art is a task somewhat beyond me, since I've remained to this day a poor man, and so have little chance to eat the sort of meals statesmen and dignitaries put on the table. I eat and devour more or less the same things the masses choke down. But why speak of choking and cramming down? A good piece of roast pork is and will always be an honest meal. Anything good enough for the populace to eat is good enough for me, like, for instance, *Sülze*, pickled meat in aspic. *Sülze* has a wonderful flavor. To be sure I find pheasant quite good as well, but a bowl of lentil soup is closer to my heart.

Translated by Susan Bernofsky

Pesto Sauce

JOHN CAGE

John Cage and Gianni Sassi in Milan (1988)

THIS IS a pesto sauce that is "macrobiotic" i.e. doesn't have cheese.

Lots of fresh basil, just the leaves
Garlic, over half a head (smash the cloves to
    make taking the paper off easier).
Pine nuts, quite a lot but to taste
Miso, two or three heaping tblsps. or more

Combine everything in a cuisinart. Then taste and
    adjust amts,
a little more of this or that, a little less being out
of the ?
Misos are all different.
Experiment, never settling on any one of them.

Saturday or Sunday Brunch

JUAN BENET

I DO NOT COOK, I do not even know how to boil an egg and hardly may I offer a recipe of my own for your book. I only dare to make a suggestion: try every two weeks, on Saturday or Sunday morning, a brunch consisting of icelandic or scandinavian marinated herrings, smoked eel, spanish "salazones" (i.e. mojama, tuna and several other roe), german sweet girkins, "serrano" ham and lots of danish beer and russian vodka. That is all. You will feel great on Saturday or Sunday afternoon.

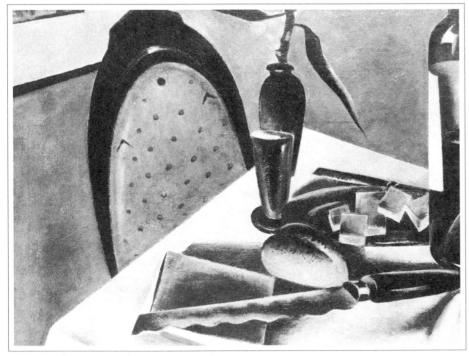

Preston Dickinson, *Still Life with Yellow Green Chair*

Lunch

GERTRUDE STEIN

LUCK IN LOOSE PLASTER makes holy gauge and nearly that, nearly more states, more states come in town light kite, blight not white.

A little lunch is a break in skate a little lunch so slimy, a west end of a board line is that which shows a little beneath so that necessity is a silk under wear. That is best wet. It is so natural, and why is there flake, there is flake to explain exhaust.

A real cold hen is nervous is nervous with a towel with a spool with real beads. It is mostly an extra sole nearly all that shaved, shaved with an old mountain, more than that bees more than that dinner and a bunch of likes that is to say the hearts of onions aim less.

Cold coffee with a corn a corn yellow and green mass is a gem.

TV Lunch Haiku

Kenward Elmslie

STEAM onion harvest.
Fry garlic in olive oil.
Add smoked ham (small chunks).
Mince coriander. Combine.
Top off with *Young and Restless.*

Sandy Skoglund, *Luncheon Meat on a Counter* (1978)

SPICES, SOUPS, SAUCES, LIGHT MEALS, LUNCHES

A Dull Poem

PAUL BLACKBURN

—ZEN FOODS
it says on the truck outside,
what can be
seen thru the bakery door
Third Avenue & 24th
where it is lunchtime
Saturday . The truck has blocked :
a young man with a portfolio from
the art school next block, he
walks very straight, proud, walked,
disappeared behind truck where
he can see, I can't,

two boys making a fire
in a can in a
vacant lot across the avenue.
Extends the depth of one building but
was an half-block of tenements
a year agone, half the way to
25th . The wood was wet, was set
before the truck came in and parked,
and smoked . No cherries here, no

mickies there. It's wet, I wonder
what there might be in that truck
—ZEN FOODS
bean sprouts and rice, all of
Chinatown's fowl & fish & vegetable,
Zen Foods, no mickies.

    Does this generation know
about mickies, set among coals, wood
fires in vacant lots, cooked to half-
raw & eaten with stolen salt / charred skins and all?
Even in those islands of still-poor Irish, their
isolated blocks about the city? No micks here
no cherries there, bean sprouts with rice &
comidas criollas composed of the obscure parts of dead pigs.
The bakery's German & serves
healthy, bland, Mitteleuropa
meals for about a buck. Tender
                    loin tomorrow
                    goulash today.
I bring my own wine.

—ZEN FOODS—

          Two elderly men
with long overcoats from third-hand shops
look at me meanly, leaving, wishing
the wine were theirs, mutter. The boys
in the lot appear throwing rocks,

broken Ignatz brick, at one another & jeering, no
micks here, no krauts there, no

Some seven-year-olds outside the plate glass
window are trying to liberate
                                   my bicycle, it
is too securely locked to a leg
of a NO PARKING sign, garnished with
        METERED PARKING and the meters as well.

They try the lamp and go see if
some eight-year-old friend has been gifted with
a screwdriver.
                 The waitress starts again
to come on, always a bit crude. That ends.
I am returned to the hopeless scene, having
                 the dollar to pay. I pay,
leave tip, the
                 —ZEN FOOD truck pulls out.
                 "How many crullers?"
                             "Two."

I do too.

Reunions and Tea

Arman, *4 O'Clock Pyramid* (1977)

Family Reunion

EUDORA WELTY

John Baldessari, *Banquet* (1988)

"JUDGE MOODY and Mrs. Moody! I hope your appetite is proving equal to the occasion," Jack was saying, while the pickled peaches and the pear relish, the five kinds of bread, the sausages and ham—fried and boiled—and the four or five kinds of salad, and the fresh crocks of milk and butter that had been pulled up out of the well, were all being set within his reach. And then Aunt Beck's chicken pie was set down spouting and boiling hot right under his nose. "Mama'll take it pretty hard if you go away leaving a scrap on your plate," he told the Moodys.

Waiting for Tea

HAROLD PINTER

Silence. GUS *shakes his head and exits.* BEN *lies back and reads. The lavatory chain is pulled once off left, but the lavatory does not flush.* BEN *whistles at an item in the paper.* GUS *re-enters.*

GUS: I want to ask you something.

BEN: What are you doing out there?

GUS: Well, I was just—

BEN: What about the tea?

GUS: I'm just going to make it.

BEN: Well, go on, make it.

GUS: Yes, I will. [*He sits in a chair. Ruminatively.*] He's laid on some very nice crockery this time, I'll say that. It's sort of striped. There's a white stripe.

BEN *reads.*

It's very nice. I'll say that.

BEN *turns the page.*

You know, sort of round the cup. Round the rim. All the rest of it's black, you see. Then the saucer's black, except for right in the middle, where the cup goes, where it's white.

BEN *reads.*

Herbie Knott, *Gilbert & George at the Market Café, London* (1987)

Then the plates are the same, you see. Only they've got a black stripe—the plates—right across the middle. Yes, I'm quite taken with the crockery.

BEN [*still reading*]: What do you want plates for? You're not going to eat.

GUS: I've brought a few biscuits.

BEN: Well, you'd better eat them quick.

GUS: I always bring a few biscuits. Or a pie. You know I can't drink tea without anything to eat.

BEN: Well, make the tea then, will you? Time's getting on.

Sugar

GERTRUDE STEIN

A VIOLENT LUCK and a whole sample and even then quiet.

Water is squeezing, water is almost squeezing on lard. Water, water is a mountain and it is selected and it is so practical that there is no use in money. A mind under is exact and so it is necessary to have a mouth and eye glasses.

A question of sudden rises and more time than awfulness is so easy and shady. There is precisely that noise.

A peck a small piece not privately overseen, not at all not a slice, not at all crestfallen and open, not at all mounting and chaining and evenly surpassing, all the bidding comes to tea.

A separation is not tightly in worsted and sauce, it is so kept well and sectionally.

Put it in the stew, put it to shame. A little slight shadow and a solid fine furnace.

The teasing is tender and trying and thoughtful.

The line which sets sprinkling to be a remedy is beside the best cold.

A puzzle, a monster puzzle, a heavy choking, a neglected Tuesday.

Wet crossing and a likeness, any likeness, a likeness has blisters, it has that and teeth, it has the staggering blindly and a little green, any little green is ordinary.

One, two and one, two, nine, second and five and that.

A blaze, a search in between, a cow, only any wet place, only this tune.

Cut a gas jet uglier and then pierce pierce in between the next and negligence. Choose the rate to pay and pet pet very much. A collection of all around, a signal poison, a lack of languor and more hurts at ease.

A white bird, a colored mine, a mixed orange, a dog.

Cuddling comes in continuing a change.

A piece of separate outstanding rushing is so blind with open delicacy.

A canoe is orderly. A period is solemn. A cow is accepted.

A nice old chain is widening, it is absent, it is laid by.

Muffins

EVELYN WAUGH

"A H , here comes tea at last," said Tony. "I hope you allow yourself to eat muffins. So many of our guests nowadays are on a diet. I think muffins one of the few things that make the English winter endurable."

"Muffins stand for so much," said Jenny.

She ate heartily; often she ran her tongue over her lips, collecting crumbs that had become embedded there and melted butter from the muffin. One drop of butter fell on her chin and glittered there unobserved except by Tony. It was a relief to him when John Andrew was brought in.

Tea Without Macaroons

ELIZABETH BOWEN

"I STARTED the kettle off from the hot tap."

They went into the kitchen, where tea was. A Dutch check cloth askew on the scrubbed table: a loaf, lump of butter, a hacked-about gâteau, less than a plateful of fancy biscuits, a pot of jam. "You should officiate, Eva?" said Mr Dancey, indicating the teapot. She retreated, askance. "I had better," suggested Henry. Grace not being said at tea-time, they sat down.

Henry, transfixing Eva, said: "Last time you were here, there were macaroons."

"Eva will make allowances," said his father.

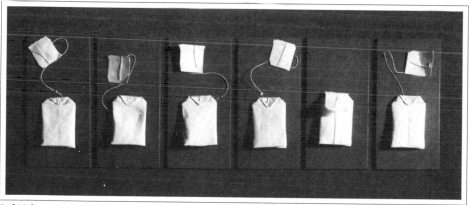

Jud Nelson, *Holos/Series 5* [*tea bags*] (1978)

Cecil Beaton, *Edith Sitwell Taking Tea in Bed* (1927)

Divertissement Exotique

JOHAN BORGEN

SHE FELT ALMOST as if she should beg his pardon, then she was confused: "Yes, but Lillelord, how did you know?"

"It's in the newspaper, Mother, every day on page four of the *Morgenbladet*. Do you know what's playing at the Bio-Cinema? 'Broken Hearts.'"

Then the laughter finally came. His mother's childish, trilling laughter that recognized only fun in the world. It was like a lid being taken off her, leaving only ineffable relief; all these mysterious things were printed every day in her own, safe *Morgenbladet*, and her gifted son, her avid little reader, had read them. And at once she seemed to have found an explanation for the indecent folk song that had agitated the prudish Misses Wollkwarts. Yes, leave them in peace, they did their best. It was as though she had to forgive a whole world now that she could forgive her beloved boy, who had only been using his sharp eyes to read the names of ships, advertisements, poems, and posters. What in the world had she been worried about?

She squeezed his thin arm, and all at once she felt she wanted to do something unusual, like in the old days, as they used to do often abroad; in the good and terribly bad, old days when her life had been a gush of days and nights, a cascade... compared to the quiet flow of a stream here in Kristiania, the calm passage of time to an old age that she seldom thought about.

"Yes, why in the world shouldn't we go to the Tivoli Theatre?" she said tentatively, but stopped herself: "But it's a long time to wait until eight o'clock."

"But Mother, don't you see? It's Saturday and there are two performances. It says so on the poster."

That too had escaped her attention. All the things she didn't see! All her boy's eyes saw and his ears heard!

"Yes, of course, it's Saturday," she said, so she wouldn't seem dumb to her quick-witted escort. They pushed to the window of the ticket office along with all the

Divertissement Exotique
Indian Fakirs' Mystical Secrets
Life in a Moorish Harem
First Time in Europe
A Teahouse in Nagasaki
Genuine Geishas

strangers, and the strange smells. They were like two lost children as they went inside and up the stairs to the theatre. A doorman in an admiral's uniform tore their tickets. Then they came to the auditorium of the theatre with its silver painted tables and chairs with curved legs. A waiter in a gleaming white apron came over, conjured a note pad out of his apron and a pencil from behind his ear.

"Have a glass of sherry, Mother," Lillelord whispered.

"A glass of sherry please," she said automatically.

"And for the young gentleman?" the waiter leaned over the table and smiled cordially.

"A glass of sherry for me too!" Lillelord whispered.

She had said it already. The waiter, naturally, had raised his eyebrows: Was she mistaken? "I think you're crazy," she said happily.

"You can easily drink two glasses of sherry," he said. She looked around furtively at the strange place. The air in the hall was thick with smoke and smells. A huge man with a roguish, beery look stepped over her feet, with his back to her, and she shivered with happiness. For some reason or other she thought of Aunt Klara and her grammatical finickiness. Lillelord was singing softly to himself amid all the noise as the theatre filled up, and tobacco smoke began to create a haze among the tables, uniting them in genial companionship.

"Lillelord, you're singing!"

He sang louder. He sang *Die Angst, die Axt* . . . to a tune he'd made up with its own rhythm.

"I was thinking of Aunt Klara!" he shouted up toward her face.

It was like lightning striking her.

"*Why* were you thinking about Aunt Klara?"

"*Die Zusammenkunft, die Feuersbrunst!*

"Don't know. Don't know...." He sang that too. He was possessed by the fever of expectation that grew with the noise around him: loud voices ordering beer and herring, drinks and meat patties and herring and beer, toddy and coffee and herring and beer.

Translated by Elizabeth Brown Moen

Cuban Tea

ORANGE SMOKE. Among tea kettles and blue cups he made out Maria's head, and those of the little Ophidia Eyes, back in their forms as chorus girls of the Opera (what happened to the Fat Ladies?), covered with stuffed humming birds, *guacamayos* and candied pineapples with rubies; also Dragon Puss, the Director, and another Chinaman, thin and wiry like an eel, bald, and mustard yellow. He was in the center of the chorus, standing and naked (yes, he had one, but small and spiraled like a little screw) next to Little Torture Face, in underpants.

The *biondas* served tea, and politely handed around sugar cubes and small pieces of grapefruit, or *lukum,* or something coated with flour.

Translated by Suzanne Jill Levine

Cocktails and Hors d'œuvres

Gerald Murphy, *Cocktail* (1927)

Whiskey & Strychnine

MALCOLM LOWRY

AND THEN the whiskey bottle: he drank fiercely from it.

He had not forgotten his glass however, and into it he was now pouring himself chaotically a long drink of his strychnine mixture, half by mistake, he'd meant to pour the whiskey. "Strychnine is an aphrodisiac. Perhaps it will take immediate effect. It still may not be too late." He had sunk through, it almost felt, the green cane rocking chair.

He just managed to reach his glass left on the tray and held it now in his hands, weighing it, but—for he was trembling again, not slightly, but violently, like a man with Parkinson's disease or palsy—unable to bring it to his lips. Then without drinking he set it on the parapet. After a while, his whole body quaking, he rose deliberately and poured, somehow, into the other unused tumbler Concepta had not removed, about a half quartern of whiskey. Nació 1820 y siguiendo tan campante. Siguiendo. Born 1896 and still going flat. I love you, he murmured, gripping the bottle with both hands as he replaced it on the tray. He now brought the tumbler filled with whiskey back to his chair and sat with it in his hands, thinking. Presently without having drunk from this glass either he set it on the parapet next to his strychnine. He sat watching both the glasses. Behind him in the room he heard Yvonne crying.

Pablo Picasso, *Glass of Absinthe* (1914)

The Impeccable Mint Julep

PAUL METCALF

A Recipe for four people, two drinks apiece

16 ounces bourbon. Heaven Hill is the preferred brand,
  although Early Times will do.
A generous supply of fresh mint leaves.
8 teaspoons Confederate Sugar. Oh, all right: *Confectioner's* Sugar.
Shaved or finely chopped ice.

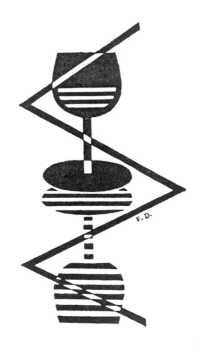

Fortunato Depero, *Campari campaign* (1931)

Chop the mint leaves. Place them in a small sauce pan, and add the sugar. Add just barely enough water to make a syrup, and bring the mixture to a rolling boil. Set aside to cool. Line up 8 highball glasses, and fill them with ice. Distribute the syrup and leaves among them, as evenly as possible. Add 2 ounces of bourbon to each glass. Stir the mixture in each glass thoroughly, with a long-handled spoon. Add more ice, as needed, to bring ice to the top of each glass. Set the glasses in the refrigerator or freezer, so that they will become frosted; this only takes a few minutes. Just before serving, place a stalk of mint in each glass.

Cheers !

The Claude Upson Daiquiri

JEROME LAWRENCE & ROBERT E. LEE

MR. UPSON: [*Pouring a daiquiri and handing it to her.*] Well, Mamie old girl, here's your poison. I make my daiquiris with a secret ingredient I learned from this native down in Havana, Cuba. You'll never guess what the secret ingredient is but I'll say this much. There's no sugar in a Claude Upson daiquiri.

> *She sips it.*

AUNTIE MAME: And yet it's so *sweet*. What *ever* do you use? Chocolate ice cream?

MR. UPSON: [*Guffawing*] Sa-a-y, that's rich. Did you hear that, Doris? Chocolate ice cream [*He puts a bearlike hand on* AUNTIE MAME's *shoulder.*] Since we're practically relatives, I'm going to let you in on my little secret, *honey.*

AUNTIE MAME: I beg your pardon?

MR. UPSON: Strained honey—that's the secret ingredient. [*He chortles.*] Of course, I use quite a little rum, too!

> MAME *points playfully into her glass and in a hail-fellow-well-met mood.*
> MRS. UPSON *comes over with a tray of canapés.*

MRS. UPSON: Now, I made these especially for you, dear.

AUNTIE MAME: [*Taking a canapé.*] Don't they look delicious, though. Mm-m-m-mm-mm-*mm*! [*She takes a bite.*] What *are* they?

MRS. UPSON: Well, I take two cans of tuna fish and put them through the meat grinder, then add clam juice and peanut butter. It's a recipe I cut out of the Ladies Home Journal. [*She proffers the other tray.*] These are just plain jack cheese and chutney. [MRS. UPSON *steers* AUNTIE MAME *to a bench. Surreptitiously,* MAME *tosses the hors d'œuvres over the patio wall.*]

Polybeverages

F.T. Marinetti

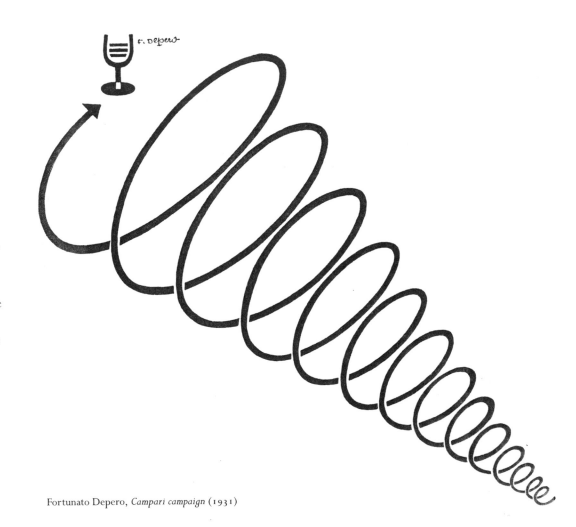

DECISION
- ¼ Chinato wine
- ¼ Rum
- ¼ Fiery Barolo
- ¼ Tangerine juice

QUICK TRICK
- ⅓ Asti spumante
- ⅓ Pineapple liqueur
- ⅓ Frozen Orange juice

Translated by Guy Bennett

Fortunato Depero, *Campari campaign* (1931)

Banana Amaze

GILBERT SORRENTINO

1 ½ oz. Gypsy Rose wine
1 oz. banana absinthe
½ oz. mastiachi pepper extract
Shake well with cracked ice and strain into a frosted cocktail glass.
Decorate with two thin rounds of ripe banana and a sprig of pink brilliantine.

"Guts" takes a sip, rolls his eyes, and grins. To the bar at large, he proclaims, "*Habits and Wimples* has nothing on this, despite its clear and complete index and exemplary notes."

Habits and Wimples?

The, ah, reference is obscure. But that's just like "Guts."

The Big Cheese

JOHN PERREAULT

The discovery of a new dish does more for the happiness of mankind than the discovery of a star.

—BRILLAT-SAVARIN

I AM a scientific genius. Or, rather, to be precise, an engineering one. Or am I a designer? I have been called all of these things. I am an inventor. That's the term I prefer. I am an inventor, like Thomas Alva Edison, although no two inventors are ever alike. But it's really true and I don't have to tell you because you've probably read it anyway. Some people think I'm right up there with Edison. You probably can tell already that I'm not particularly modest. All I can say is this: I've come up with a lot of good ideas. And all my products, conveniences, and improvements have added a lot to people's lives and made me rich in the process.

Well, let's put it this way: I have ideas, ideas that can be turned into profits, and

I have a way with things, of making an idea concrete and giving it cash value. After my first big-payoff inventions or discoveries, I didn't even need a way with things; I got myself a staff. One invention led to another. The money kept pouring in; it still does. All I really ever needed was ideas, and I have never had a lack of those.

What is my secret? I start with myself. That's my first million-dollar idea. What would I really like? What do I need? What would make my life better, even a little bit better? What would I pay good money for? What would make my life more comfortable and pleasurable?

There's a lecture I give, and I've given it all over the country and in Europe, too, that I call "How To Invent Your Way To Big Money." What I've just said is exactly how I begin it every time. Usually I make people pay big bucks for these words; I only speak to twenty people at a time and I charge them each $1,000 at least. My time is valuable to me. I have to say, though, that most people just don't get the message no matter how

much they pay to hear me speak. Most people are lumps. So you can quote me for free. I figure that poor people might do better with my secret to success than the rich ones.

If you want to know more about me, you can look me up in *Who's Who*. There you'll find my companies listed. I forget a lot of them myself because it's something my accountants and lawyers take care of. But there they also list my honorary degrees and all my awards. But they don't tell you that I came from humble beginnings.

I was born in New Jersey, the Jersey Shore, that narrow piece of vacation that stretches from Keansburg to Cape May, made up of tacky boardwalks, merry-go-rounds, and miniature golf. The suckers from North Jersey came down on the Fourth and left on Labor Day, leaving behind dirty cottages—my mother used to clean those cottages—littered beaches, filthy, beer cans everywhere.

It was dull, particularly if you lived there all year round. To make matters worse, when I was old enough to be able to miss the ocean when it wasn't there, my family moved inland to where the chicken farms were and it was too far to walk to the beach. There was sand, but it had briars growing out of it and not much else. It wasn't even very dramatic the way it gets further south, where it becomes the Pine Barrens.

Even then I was lazy. It must have been just after World War Two. It was before housing developments and garbage collection. I remember I didn't want to bury the garbage, which was one of my chores, so I invented a garbage liquefier using parts from my mother's old Mix-Master and other things. It worked. It made a lot of noise and then you hosed the liquid down the kitchen sink. Of course the cesspool eventually backed up, but then I figured a way around that, too.

I finished high school and then just hung around. There never'd been any possibility of going to college. My grades were not good enough; guess I was a dreamer. Most things in high school bored me. So I was saved from college. I wish I could say it was a narrow escape, but it wasn't. My mother and father never had any money. Still, I was lucky, judging by some of the college

people that turn up thinking I'll hire them for one of my laboratories and they don't know a thing. You practically have to teach them how to pick their noses.

Right out of high school, I spent my spare time inventing things. I never did quite figure out how to make a self-dissolving beer can. Still can't. But I did invent a few wild things: a crazy automatic tulip bulb planter, cups with permanent saucers, a mailbox sensor, self-folding maps, dust bunny magnets. Here and there and now and then I worked at odd jobs, knowing that eventually I would invent something that would make a lot of money. I was a short-order cook, really a hot-dog man, on the Asbury Park boardwalk; I was a bumpercar attendant; I was an usher in a seaside movie theater. I worked for a company that bought used frying fat from luncheonettes.

One thing led to another. I moved from home, got away from my mother and father. One of them died and the other one was too crazy to put up with and so there was no one left but me, as I had no brothers or sisters. I had my own little trailer in the woods and then a cinder-block laboratory right next to it. At first not much came out of my lab. But

one day I was all out of matches and I'd lost my cigarette lighter. Of course, there was no one else around for miles. I was a loner; still am. I was desperate for a smoke. I had plenty of cigarettes but no way to light one up. I finally remembered that the gas heater had a pilot light somewhere underneath and inside of it. So I used that. But it made me think that it would be wonderful to have cigarettes that wouldn't need matches or lighters. Self-lighting cigarettes. Their tips could be matches and the striking surface could be right on the package. I worked on the idea for two years, perfected it, and then sold it to Philip Morris. "A great contribution to humanity," said the president of Philip Morris. I think he got carried away. Nevertheless, where would we be without self-lighting cigarettes? Searching for matches, that's where.

My next big killing was the Temp-Tub. You turn it on and it fills itself up with water at the temperature you prefer and the temperature stays that way, no matter how long you soak. This is how the Temp-Tub came about: I got my best ideas while soaking in a bathtub. Still do. A real bathtub was the first thing I bought for my trailer in the woods when I got my first royalty payment from Philip Morris. The bathtub almost filled the trailer, but it was worth it. But the water kept cooling down too fast. It is cold in the woods when you only have a trailer between you and the woods. So I invented the Temp-Tub; it just took thermostats and a heating device; the rest is history. I am always my own first customer.

Next I discovered sex. Why had it taken so long? I didn't have time for it or maybe I just needed to wait for the wrong person. But, along with discovering sex, I also discovered that I didn't like ice-cold lubricant. Why was K.Y. always ice cold? You could balance the tube on a lampshade of a lit lamp, if you were planning ahead. Or leave it on a nearby radiator, but then the goo might get too hot. Why not have tubes of lubricant that produced the stuff at body temperature right out of the tube? Another great idea.

My first efforts involved battery-equipped tube cases and plug-in containers. But, I thought, who wants to fool around with tube cases, batteries, and containers? So while shaving one day, I suddenly remembered self-heating shaving cream. I remembered I was fascinated by it as a child. I used to watch my father shave. One day he left it on the sink where I could reach it. He wasn't around. I covered myself with it and when my mother found me, I was severely punished. I was not allowed to go to my room all day….

How did self-heating shaving cream work? I put the members of my staff to work. Did anyone have the patent? The solution to the ice-cold lubricant problem had come in a flash, and I became a multi-millionaire almost overnight, a billionaire. From Temp-Tub to Temp-Tube.

I like inventing and I like making money. Others dream, I produce. I like adding to my own pleasures and comforts by adding to the pleasures and comforts of others, or vice versa. It's made me famous.

Now, however, I have come to like my privacy. No more talk shows, no more lectures. I'm giving you this interview because after you wrote to me, I looked you up and I like what you've written: articles about free enterprise, interviews with captains of industry and successful artists, think pieces about the creative spirit and the need for individualism. Also, at this late date, I have a new product. It is my best invention yet. It's going to be difficult for the public to swallow so, although I am a shy person and value my newfound privacy, I need all the publicity I can get. None of my companies wants to mass-produce my new product. I am now at the stage where my companies seem to control me. How did that happen? I still don't understand.

It's a new kind of cheese. Maybe my companies don't like it because it is really not a convenience item, but instead a new luxury, a new taste, one I find addictive. I'm going to let you try some, but not yet. I want to tell you about it first. It's there on the table, on the silver tray under the silver dome.

Where shall I begin? I'll begin with the part you probably don't know. After my Temp-Tub and my Temp-Tube and a few other inventions, I felt I had enough money to retire. Some of my inventions are still Top Secret and the military is keeping them under wraps. Maybe that's why I retired from public life, out of disgust. Pleasure is more important than death. I have always been patriotic, so it was easy for them to get to me and convince me that they needed my help. I helped them figure out how pleasure can be used as a secret weapon. I think they

Mel Ramos, *Val Veeta* (1965)

enough of it in the old days. I could buy anyone I wanted and could pay enough so they would do anything I wanted. I even fell in love once or twice, which, of course, was against my better judgment. But, you know, something was always missing.

This leads me to another invention of mine. This is secret information, too. I invented the sex machine. I made the first one for myself. Inflatable dolls and masturbation devices were never enough for me—those sex-toy things, wasn't that what they used to call them? Now everyone uses the Sexomach, or Mack. If you can't afford to buy one, you can rent one. It doesn't look like a person at all, but it does all the things a person can do, only better. Now if that isn't a gift to humanity, I don't know what is. It has had a very soothing, calming effect, I think you'll agree. People aren't always pawing at each other, and it's more hygienic. Fits in a briefcase, has a passive and an active mode.

Not too long ago I tried sex with a person again, just for old time's sake. When I finally found someone who remembered how to do it—he was even older than me, a holdout—and we did it, it was so boring and mechanical that

are already using these inventions of mine in other countries, but I'm not sure. Pleasure is a way to control other people. The pleasures of revolution and killing are nothing compared to the pleasure-weapons I have invented. But I am not allowed to talk about these things. Some day the whole truth will come out, and this unprecedented period of worldwide peace will be explained, long af-

ter I am dead, when they won't have me to contradict whatever reasoning they use.

So, to make a long story short, I didn't need any more money. How much money can one person use? Two things became my only joy: sex and food.

I hope I won't embarrass you by talking about sex, but I never seemed to get

COCKTAILS AND HORS D'ŒUVRES

I knew for certain what a boon my Mack has been. It's subtle, inventive, cheaper, and infinitely adaptable. I was right to put it on the market.

But I have outgrown the Mack. You probably find that hard to believe, but after many years with the first model and then working on and developing all the improved models—as I said before, I always start with myself—I am not at all interested any more. My interest in food, however, has continued and deepened. Sex with one of my sex machines, if you play it right, if you surrender, can leave you sexually satisfied for days, weeks, and sometimes months. You don't even want to think about sex. Food, on the other hand, is a constant. The satisfaction you get from food, even the most rarefied food, lasts only four hours. Then you need more. Divorcing taste from hunger, as I have been able to do, presents an even more insatiable situation.

Food, like sex, was always there, but more or less in the background. A bite to eat, a ceremonial lunch or supper. But after I retired it came to the foreground. I found at last the craving, the desire that could not be satisfied: the need for a new taste. I went from American to French to Chinese to Mexican to Japanese to Thai. I tried to eat everything there is to eat, save human flesh. That is my limit. I have tasted every wine. I have reconstructed historical cuisines.

I became obsessed with finding the perfect food. I found it. That perfect food is cheese. It offers more variety and richness than wine, meats, or all fruits, grains, and vegetables combined. Like wine, it is made. Like wine, its basic steps of manufacture are simple and profound, but even more than wine, the tastes diverge and multiply. You do this by altering one of several factors. Choosing the milk and curdling it, straining the curds and draining and pressing them. Salt. Then, if you want, the introduction of bacteria. And yet, unlike wine, the results are so solid, so material, so physical.

I began to think that this perfect and, yes, most poetic of foods was the true food of the gods and that there must be one cheese on earth that is the most perfect of all. I tasted all of the cheeses of the world. I tasted the most perfect of each: Bel Paese, Caprice des Dieux, Caerphilly, Cheshire, and all the rest. I settled on the blues: Bleu d'Auvergne, Bleu de Bresse, Bleu de Causses, Bleu du Haut-Jura, Blue Castello, Blue Norwegian, Danablue, Fourme d'Ambert, Gammelost, Gorgonzola, Mycella, Pipo Crem, Roquefort, and, glory of glories, Stilton, the King. I even hunted down the legendary Blue Vinny. How many times has this name been used in vain, how many frauds have been committed? What we found was strange but true. Blue Vinny, true Blue Vinny, disappeared when laws were passed forbidding the making of cheese in barns with livestock. The blue mold in Blue Vinny had come from horse harnesses dipped in the milk each night.

I hired historians. I bought some land in Dorset, had an entire barnyard reconstructed. It cost a fortune, but after five years I managed to produce an authentic Blue Vinny. Dipped the harnesses myself. I produced a fine and luxurious Blue, not as good as a Stilton, but distinct.

I was not satisfied. What next? My turophilia had no bounds.

As you no doubt have already guessed, my need to invent returned. I could no longer be passive. Stilton, no matter how majestic, is not enough. My newfound love of cheese and my love of inventing came together. I decided to invent or, at the very least, discover a new taste. Cheese, I determined, was the perfect medium. There were variables that one could alter and control in a logical way. I was successful; the results are on that silver platter under the silver dome.

I put my technicians to work on the various molds; the workable ones were few in number and the forced mutations did not pan out. The other big variable is, of course, the kind of milk you use. So I asked myself an important question. Cheese has been made from cow milk, sheep milk, buffalo milk, even camel milk and yak milk. What else is there?

Shall I give you my list? I was limited out of necessity to mammals. I have made and have tasted cheese made from the milk of the following animals: cats, dogs, whales, bears, wolves, elephants, horses, porpoises, tigers. We did not succeed in producing a new taste. We thought we had something with dolphin but, even with the introduction of various molds, it always ended up tasting like Gorgonzola, bad Gorgonzola.

Human milk came next. Ugh. It was different, but not new. It recalled my mother's milk, this slightly salty cheese. Naturally salty. I then determined that

to have a new taste, not only did I have to have a new cheese, but a new milk to make that new cheese. In other words, if I can be clear, new cheese can only be made from new milk.

In one of those great poetic leaps—like the leap from my father's shaving cream to Temp-Tube—I jumped from mother's milk to father's milk. Male milk was the answer. I had thought of disinterring my father and allowing my lab men to grow breasts from the remaining tissues and force lactation with various hormones and light treatments. But we could not find his grave. I found some teenage boys who were willing to comply with my experiments. I paid them a great deal. There are cases on record of males who have lactated; even nursed infants. All it takes is the proper hormones.

Teenage milk, alas, makes a teenage cheese.

I needed a real man, an adult male.

I returned to first principles. I always start with myself. I took the hormones and other treatments. I grew breasts. I became Tiresias. When we had enough milk, we made the cheese. I tasted it. It was new. It *is* new. It is on that silver platter under the silver dome. I would like you to taste it. I find it wonderful. And

yet, I am haunted by a terrible question: is it only a new taste to me because it is the cheese of my very own milk? Because, in a sense, I am eating myself. To experience this new taste, will each man have to make a cheese from his own milk? Is all male milk the same? Or does the new taste come only from me?

Here, taste it. I'll let you decide.

Oysters

ELIZABETH BOWEN

Patrick Caulfield, *Still Life: Autumn Fashion* (1978)

ISEULT'S ENJOYMENT of her oysters was at once methodical and voluptuous. The very first she swallowed wrought a change in her. Greed softened and in a peculiar way spiritualized her abstruse beauty, with its touch of the schoolroom. Eating became her—more than once she had been fallen in love with over a meal. She gave herself up, untainted, to this truest sensuality that she knew. Her nonchalance with the menu had been a feint; or more, a prudishness as to her deeper nature—of which the revelation was so surprising, so at variance with the Iseult that had been, as to be first intriguing, then disturbing, then in itself seductive ... How she ate, Eric had ceased to notice; and Constantine did not care.

The Oyster

FRANCIS PONGE

THE OYSTER, the size of an average pebble, has a coarser appearance, a less even color, brilliantly whitish. It is a stubbornly closed world. It can be opened however: you have to hold it in the hollow of a rag, use a chipped, rather dull knife and go at it several times. Curious fingers are cut, nails broken: it's a rough job. Nicking it, we mark its casing with white circles, sorts of halos.

Inside we find an entire world, to eat and drink: under a pearly *firmament* (strictly speaking), the skies above merge with the skies below, forming a single pool, a viscous, greenish sachet that flows back and forth to both smell and sight, and that is fringed with a blackish lace.

On very rare occasions a little form beads in their pearly throats, with which we quickly adorn ourselves.

Translated by Guy Bennett

Oysters, Caviar, Sour Pickles & Sausages

Junichirō Tanizaki

"The old one" cleared the table, and covered it afresh with the food she had brought: oysters, caviar, sour pickles, pork and chicken and liver sausages, and again all sorts of bread. The drinking began: vodka and beer were brought out, and heated saké, in drinking glasses rather than the tiny cups more commonly used. Of the Russians, "the old one" and Katharina seemed fond of saké. There was, as Teinosuke had feared, not room for all of them to sit down. Katharina leaned against the mantle, and "the old one" helped herself from behind the rest when she was not busy bringing out new dishes. Since there were not enough knives and forks, Katharina sometimes picked something up in her hand. She turned scarlet when one of the guests caught her. They had to pretend not to notice.

"Stay away from the oysters," Sachiko whispered to Teinosuke. The oysters showed every sign of being not deep-sea oysters, but quite ordinary oysters picked up at a near-by fish market. The Russians, who ate them with great gusto, were on that point, at least, not as discriminating as their Japanese guests.

Translated by Edward G. Seidensticker

Olive Pâté

BLAISE CENDRARS

At hand

Jars of olives along the far wall of the farmhouse kitchen
A food mill clamped onto the edge of the kitchen table
A ladle
A fork
A ham, a salami, a plait of garlic hanging from a rafter
A frying pan
A big round loaf of bread.

Recipe (Provençal)

Roll up your sleeves
Ladle up green and black olives, mild, bitter, and salty, from the jars
Pit
Dump pitted olives into mill and turn the handle while singing
Pour into the frying pan and make them sizzle in their own oil
Serve boiling hot, with a hunk of bread, some salami and ham, while
telling jokes and tickling the garlic cloves with the three prongs of your fork
Take your time eating, while drinking the local wine ad lib
Wash it all down with pale ale. Then you smoke a pipe or
roll a cigarette.

Translated by Ron Padgett

COCKTAILS AND HORS D'ŒUVRES

On the Sideboard

VLADIMIR NABOKOV

AT THIS MOMENT both battants of the door were flung open by Bouteillan in the grand manner, and Demon offered *kalachikom* (in the form of a Russian crescent loaf) his arm to Marina. Van, who in his father's presence was prone to lapse into a rather dismal sort of playfulness, proposed taking Ada in, but she slapped his wrist away with a sisterly *sans-gêne,* of which Fanny Price might not have approved.

Another Price, a typical, too typical, old retainer whom Marina (and G. A. Vronsky, during their brief romance) had dubbed, for unknown reasons, "Grib," placed an onyx ashtray at the head of the table for Demon, who liked to smoke between courses—a puff of Russian ancestry. A side table supported, also in the Russian fashion, a collection of red, black, gray, beige hors d'œuvres, with the serviette caviar (*salfetochnaya ikra*) separated from the pot of Graybead (*ikra svezhaya*) by the succulent pomp of preserved boletes, "white," and "subbetuline," while the pink of smoked salmon vied with the incarnadine of Westphalian ham. The variously flavored *vodochki* glittered, on a separate tray. The French cuisine had contributed its *chaudfroids* and *foie gras.* A window was open, and the crickets were stridulating at an ominous speed in the black motionless foliage.

Little Cambray Tamales

For Eduardo and Helena who asked me for a Salvadoran recipe

CLARIBEL ALEGRIA

(makes 5,000,000 little tamales)

Two pounds of mestizo cornmeal
half a pound of loin of *gachupin*
cooked and finely chopped
a box of pious raisins
two tablespoons of Malinche milk
one cup of enraged water
a fry of conquistador helmets
three Jesuit onions
a small bag of multinational gold
two dragon's teeth
one presidential carrot
two tablespoonsful of pimps
lard of Panchimalco Indians
two ministerial tomatos
a half cup of television sugar
two drops of volcanic lava
seven leaves of *pito*
(don't be dirty-minded, it's a soporific)
put everything to boil
over a slow fire
for five hundred years
and you'll see what a flavor it has.

Translated by Darwin J. Hakoll

COCKTAILS AND HORS D'ŒUVRES

Vegetables

Photographer unknown

Mean Beans, Rice & Greens Joeritta

FANNY HOWE

OIL, garlic, brown or white rice, water, bag of beans, bay leaf, salt, and collard greens.

Saute the rice in a heavy pot or pan, saute it with a little oil, two crushed garlic cloves and salt, until each grain is well coated with the oil. Then cover the rice with boiling water and bring to another boil; cover, lower heat and simmer adding more hot water until the rice is cooked.

Having soaked the black or kidney beans overnight, cook in deep water with a bay leaf and no other seasoning. Keep adding water and hold it at a simmer until the beans are soft and not too thick. Then saute two crushed garlic cloves in oil with a teaspoon of salt. When the garlic is brown, add a cup of beans to that pan and stir around until mixed. Then pour that mixture back into the big pot of beans to season it.

To clean the greens, wash each leaf separately, having cut off the stems. Roll two or three leaves lengthwise into a kind of tube and slice crosswise ultra-thin, thinner than cole slaw! In a pan saute two crushed garlic cloves in oil and salt. Add the greens and stir fry over a low heat until the greens are bright green.

Serve beans on rice with greens beside and a bottle of hot sauce too.

Asparagus

MARCEL PROUST

WHEN I WOULD GO downstairs to find out what was for dinner, it was already being prepared, and Françoise, commanding the forces of nature which had become her assistants, as in fairy tales when giants are employed as cooks, would be poking at the coal, setting the potatoes to steam, and putting the finishing touches on culinary masterpieces first prepared in a variety of ceramic receptacles going from great vats, pots, cauldrons and fish kettles, to terrines for game, pastry molds and little cream pitchers, having passed through an entire collection of saucepans of all sizes. I would stop at the table to see the peas which the kitchen girl had just shelled, all lined up and numbered like the green marbles in a game; but my greatest pleasure was the asparagus, bathed in ultramarine and pink and whose spears, delicately brushed in mauve and azure, fade imperceptibly to the base of the stalk—still soiled with the earth of their bed—through iridescences that are not of this world. It seemed to me that these celestial nuances betrayed the delicious creatures that had amused themselves by becoming vegetables and which, through the disguise of their firm, edible flesh, gave a glimpse in these dawn born colors, these rainbow sketches, this extinction of blue evenings, of the precious essence that I would still recognize when, all night following a dinner where I had eaten them, they played in their crude, poetic farces, like one of Shakespeare's fairies, at changing my chamberpot into a bottle of perfume.

Translated by Guy Bennett

Tomates à la crème

TAKE SIX TOMATOES. Cut them in halves. In your frying pan melt a lump of butter. Put in the tomatoes, cut side downwards, with a sharply pointed knife puncturing here and there the rounded sides of the tomatoes. Let them heat for five minutes. Turn them over. Cook them for another ten minutes. Turn them again. The juices run out and spread into the pan. Once more turn the tomatoes cut side upwards. Around them put 80 grams (3 oz. near enough) of thick cream. Mix it with the juices. As soon as it bubbles, slip the tomatoes and all their sauce onto a hot dish. Serve instantly, very hot.

This is an adaptation of a recipe of Edou de Pomaine, who was famous in Franc or his ideas about cooking, mainly expre in a radio program of the Thirties. Pom was Polish or half-Polish, and is said t ve got this recipe from his Polish mother.

Bart Parker, *Tomatoe Picture* (1977)

Peas

MARTHA RONK

FOOD IN THE FORM of princesses sleeping on twenty mattresses to find out, or what saints digest in their dreams. A wafer as thin as skin as the pea is hard. Some people have thin skins.

Some parents are accused of equating food with love; if it were only as easy as getting some chocolate sprinkling it with chocolate and spreading it with a flat knife.

In the marketplace of ideas some prefer risotto which can also be served with peas for color. Which isn't to say this isn't a good idea or even an idea about cultures though not this one.

As a child growing up in Ohio a place some equate with American simplicity and stupidity but which at the time I thought of as what is, I ate creamed peas and potatoes; I don't remember at all what this dish tasted like and I haven't had it since, but I do remember the shape of things in the mouth rolling around. Children today also seem to like frozen peas, how they stick together with small bits of ice and how they have to be pounded first to fit in the saucepan. My mother says I also ate fistfuls of sand from the sandbox. As I recall, an otherworldly experience. The best I have ever had were eaten raw standing in a row of peas in a garden in Readsboro, Vermont; they were also good cooked just then quickly in a bit of water with a bit of butter, but not so good.

In a movie in which the two are played as a couple, Dr. Watson doesn't want Holmes to interrupt him as he finishes eating his dinner which includes a few peas he is chasing around his plate; how-ever, Holmes smashes them on a fork so they can get on with it. "Bloody rude, squashing a fellow's pea." My sympathies are with the detective. Eating seems, except for saints, a waste of time, or at least a hindrance to getting on with a vision or the ball. What either of those might be, is a more difficult question.

Historical Implications of Turnips

bpNichol

turnips are

inturps are

urnspit are

tinspur are

rustpin are

stunrip are

piturns are

ritpuns are

punstir are

nutrips are

suntrip are

untrips are

spinrut are

runspit are

pitnurs are

turnsip are

tipruns are

turpsin are

spurtin

A Text on Corn

JOSÉ CORONEL URTECHO

BUT THE INDIGENOUS BASIS of Nicaraguan cuisine is none of those things previously enumerated—it is neither meat nor fish (however indisputable may be the reliance of the Indian upon the yield of his fisherman's nets and hunter's snares)—it is, rather, corn. Corn was the sustenance, the diet, the work, the life, the religion of the Indian. It was the gift of his ancient gods, which he disseminated throughout his country. And so it still is—if not the entire foundation, it remains the better part of Nicaraguan cuisine. It has been subject, naturally enough, to Creole influences, and has given birth, in turn, to many new Mestizo recipes, but despite its varied adaptations, it has essentially kept and little diverged from its prehistoric forms of preparation. Assigning new names to dishes having indigenous recipes based on corn seems strange, because it is plainly evident that almost all of these recipes existed long before being called as such and, what is more, so many of these names seem foreign to the character and original purpose of the dishes whose recipes they represent. The foodstuffs created with these recipes are portable meals, that is to say, meals which can be carried in handbaskets or other compact containers, or which could simply be held in the hand by their edible wrappers, a practice quite common in village societies agrarian since long ago, but constantly on the move, and always liable to migration. In fact, it was because of this, that the tortilla came to be pressed into service as a wrapper, to form neat little parcels of food, such as the tamale, each with its own envelope, or, similarly, why it became so popular to transport small portions of cereal or corn meal in chocolate cups, jugs, or hollow gourds. All these containers and others, for grain, for garden vegetables, and for fruit, comprise the cargo slung over the back of the Indian as he takes his merchandise to market. It was in this fashion, principally, that maize and all its comestible derivatives came to permeate every facet of Nicaraguan cuisine. Even in sopa de pobre* one finds cobs, and husks, and ears of green corn, which are, in and of themselves, nourishing food. But the primogeniture of maize is the tortilla. Its form is a miracle of functional perfection attained by a race of plastic artists who repeatedly found it necessary to rid themselves of receptacles when eating in the fields or along the roads. The tortilla is at one and the same time a plate, a meal, and a spoon or scoop. It can be eaten by itself or can accompany other foods. Consequently, it is the perfect everyday food, not only for the Indian, but for the Nicaraguan populace in general. Bread never quite managed to displace the tortilla from her native realm but, on the contrary, saw the tortilla occupy all the tables which were his by right, and sat by his side at the table's head, like a conquistador with his native wife.

---

* "Sopa de pobre": literally, "poor man's soup" = hobo stew; mulligan stew

Until the introduction of modern commercial bakeries, bread slid out of Nicaraguan ovens home-baked, as if by artisans. It was unbeatable, almost as good as in Europe, but without wheat flour being produced in the country in sufficient quality and quantity, its consumption depended, to a large extent, just as did that of wine and oil, upon the lures and pitfalls of commerce, and it didn't take root, like the tortilla, among popular tastes and customs. Nevertheless, there is no shortage in Nicaragua of an infinity of sweets, of those items known in the occident as bakery goods: of meat pies, and fritters, glazed doughnuts, muffins, crackers, biscuits, cookies, blintzes, spiced buns, layer cakes, caramel rolls, and all the other Creole variants on the traditional pastries of Europe. But dainties, sweets, and delicacies made from maize—doughnuts, creampuffs, fruitcakes—were more appealing to the Mestizo palate, by virtue of their earthy flavor and, among their other charms, tasted better with chocolate or with porridge. In the arena of the afternoon snack, as a further testimony to its nourishment, the tortilla once again is seen to dominate, not only in the form of gallitos—quarters or halves of tortillas adorned with cheese, beans, or meat, but transformed by a touch of indigenous or Mestizo fantasy, into revueltas, rellenos, or yoltascas.* Significantly, the yoltasca kept its Nahuatl name while the tortilla exchanged hers for a Castillian one, and took on a meaning which the Nicaraguan Indians never meant to give it prior to the Conquest. This can be explained, in certain fashion, because the tortilla converted itself into the bread of the village, while the yoltasca, less simple, but still basically a tortilla, made with sifted corn flour—was relegated to a position of lesser importance and assumed the status appropriate to the occasional snack.

Corn makes, what is more, the tamales—the tamal pisque, tamales rellenos or revueltos, nacatamales and yol-tamales—which are also light meals, suitable for being sold at outdoor stands, and convenient for taking on trips, hikes, and picnics. The tamal pisque is the only one of them which has been preserved in its indigenous purity, in its ancient condition as a primary, manual foodstuff—like bread and the tortilla—with its very dense, fresh dough free from grease or juices which sweat through. Thus it is easy to handle, and can be partitioned again and again. No food is more practical for use by nomadic tribes, troops, or prisoners. A tamale with a tuco or a lump of cheese has enjoyed currency in Nicaragua since colonial times, and makes a simple, frugal ration. In the villages, one is forever hearing: tamale con queso, comida de preso.* These elementary commodities—bread, the tortilla, the plantain, the tamal—each an obligatory accompaniment to all the others, are known in Nicaragua by a special word meaning "staple." And certainly, it seems sensible enough that the name given during the Conquest to staples or ingestable provisions for equestrian expeditions was restricted to those foods easiest to transport and allocate. Nicaragua, what is more, must be acknowledged as one of the countries with the widest variety of staples. Until only a few years ago, custom called for bread with breakfast,

---

*"Revueltas, rellenos, yoltascas": sorts of turnovers, omelettes, or fricasees.

*"Tamale con queso, comida de preso" = "Tamale with cheese, a guard jingling keys": food served in jail; an inmate's dinner; prisoner's fare

plantain with lunch, and tortilla with dinner. But there recurs in meals and snacks all the year round, a broad gamut of selection, from roasted bananas and tamales, to the least prestigious guinea fowl. Everything went well with beans which, over a long period of time, became the compulsory meal for the villager. He spent his life working to earn his frijoles.

The originators of Nicaraguan cuisine invented the most elaborate, fanciful, and felicitous methods of preparation, though the simplest cook with his ladle full of juice, was abundantly skillful and just as much at home with a meal of tortillas, as with a succulent soup. The inedible beans which are doled out, in pellet form, to the peons at not a few haciendas symbolize the gravest result of a decay of the national cuisine, which has paralleled the dissolution of society. Good society and good cuisine always go hand in hand. When the state of the country was healthy, rice was plentiful

and never left beans unescorted, meat was abundant and any cut was available, tortillas never seen without cheese for companion. After three centuries of successful cattle-breeding and dairy development, Nicaragua inherited the magnificent cheeses which it has to this day. It would be difficult to find better cheeses anywhere than the lion-flower or palm frond cheeses; salted cheeses; smoked cheeses; dry milk cheeses that must be cut with a saw but melt in the mouth, just the same; cheeses oily with butter, with perfume, with the ambient odors and flavors of the hacienda; and the fresh, frothy butter, white and labile, for eating with baked bananas. And the curds for the tortillas…These were the finest delicacies of the colonial haciendas and of the Nicaraguan table, where the families used to regale themselves with indigenous beverages made from maize: tiste and pinolillo, stirred with almost ritual precision right in each person's goblet; a still lighter

pinol, the sifted pinol powder for the sick and the convalescent; tibio for the old folks, and even posol for women who were nursing. The other indigenous drink, that made from cacao, which was the theobroma of the aboriginal gods, supplied the chocolate for refreshments mixed with water or with milk which, along with tortilla and curds, was the choice of most grandmothers at suppertime. If one of them had had the happy occasion to pen her culinary memoirs, an entire book would have been required to hold them, and that at the very least! It would be impossible to list, in this elegy, the national dishes created with vegetables and fruits of the earth. A separate chapter would have to be allotted to each vegetable and each fruit: the ayote, the chayote,* the pipian, the jocote and, above all else, a chapter devoted to the aguacate. Even the humble quelite leaf, finely chopped and fricaseed in corn meal with bits of pineapple, ginger, and banana, or used to

*"Ayote and chayote": types of squash; ayote pumpkinlike, chayote green

season pork ribs cut into thin strips, produced some of the most distinctive Mestizo dishes having indigenous antecedents, as did the ayaco, or agiaco, whose name has become synonymous with medley or mixture. Like all truly Nicaraguan foods, ayaco is another symbol of the Mestizo marketplace.

This interminable banquet cannot be brought to a close, however, without a brief tip of the hat to the desserts. The confectionery of Nicaragua has always been rich and varied, like the rest of its cuisine. Sweet gruel, sour fruit gruel, licorice pulp, rice pudding, jellies and jams, tarts, cottage cheese, molasses candy, melon paste, waffles and cereal squares, cupcakes, caramels, gossamer chocolate, sugarplums, nut brittle, candied fruits, layer cakes, pastels, cream puffs, spiced buns, and every other sort of pastry; flaky things, spun things, washed down with cinnamon wine and other cool refreshments: an infinity of dainties, delicacies, and sweet delights,

each springing forth according to its root, whether on the sunny ranches of the Indians with their patient cheese tubs, or in the vineyards and dank cellars of the remotest monastery, in bakeries or in taverns, the corner shop or marketplace stall. It can be said of all the fruits and many of the vegetables and grains, that if they weren't desserts in themselves, they were divine for making syrups and preserves, tarts, and beverages. In the sweet-shops of the past one envisions mile-long tables or rows of tables covered with pitchers of cocoa or milk, sweet potato, papaya, cider, rice, bitter oranges and grapefruit, pineapple and sapoyol pie. With mangos, mammees, jocotes, cashews, currants, papayas, figs, amaryllis blossoms and rapeseed oil, all mixed together in a clay basin or, better still, for greater refinement, each fruit separated in sugar preserves and mixed afterwards, to make one of the most endemic of desserts, curbasa, the presentation of which

has nowadays become the rule during Holy Week. To alleviate the rigors of the climate, Nicaragua offers the best natural refreshments in the world: chicha made with corn or sour grapes, horchata made from rice or from jicaro seed, chingues, posoles; and nectars, really soothing and delicious, which are distilled from fruits, nuts, seeds and grains, such as barley, cottonseed, pine nuts, pomegranates, oranges, lemons, tamarind, pitaya, cashews, or the truly exquisite guava. With a few exceptions, all these beverages date back to colonial times, but the golden age arrived in this century with the manufacture of ice in the country, and already we can see, in this era of refrigeration, however briefly it has been upon us, that the traditional beverages are becoming rapidly displaced by coke machines and soda fountains.

Translated by Gilbert Alter-Gilbert

Onion Pie

PAUL AUSTER

In 1973–74, my girlfriend and I were caretakers in an old farmhouse in the South of France. Deep in the back country of Provence, surrounded by vineyards and lavender fields, we lived in almost total isolation for an entire year. The nearest village was on top of a cliff, a good half hour away. Its population was forty.

The owners of the house gave us a minuscule monthly salary which we supplemented by translating art books for a publisher in Paris. For the first few months, we managed to squeak by, but during one painful stretch toward the end of winter, we found ourselves without any money at all. A check was supposedly in the mail for us, but it did not come. Bit by bit, we ate our way through the food in the cupboards and wondered what would happen to us.

In the end, we had a sack of onions, some cooking oil, and a pre-made pie crust that the owners had left behind the previous summer. The natural solution was to bake an onion pie, and so we went ahead and prepared it, chopping onions and carefully placing them in the crust. Then we put the whole business into the oven and waited for it to cook.

No food has ever tasted better to me. Because it was the end, because it was the last meal we could ever count on eating, the onion pie had a holiness to it that transcended the realm of mere food. Delicious, we said to each other, chewing as slowly as possible, but after two or three bites we were forced to admit that the pie was cold in the center and needed a little more cooking time.

We put it back in the oven and then went outside for a walk around the house, thinking that the minutes would pass more quickly that way. We walked briskly, as I remember, and did not dawdle as we made our circuit around the old stone house. When we returned to the kitchen, however, we found that the pie had been charred beyond recognition. We did our best to eat it, but it was inedible.

We spent the rest of the day talking about what we would do next. We talked and talked, but nothing came of our conversation except fear. That evening, a friend drove up to the house unannounced, and when we told him that we were out of food and money, he took us to a hotel five miles away and bought us dinner. It was a superb meal, complete with appetizers, desserts, and several bottles of Bordeaux, but for all the pleasure it gave me, it couldn't compare to those bites of onion pie I had eaten earlier in the day.

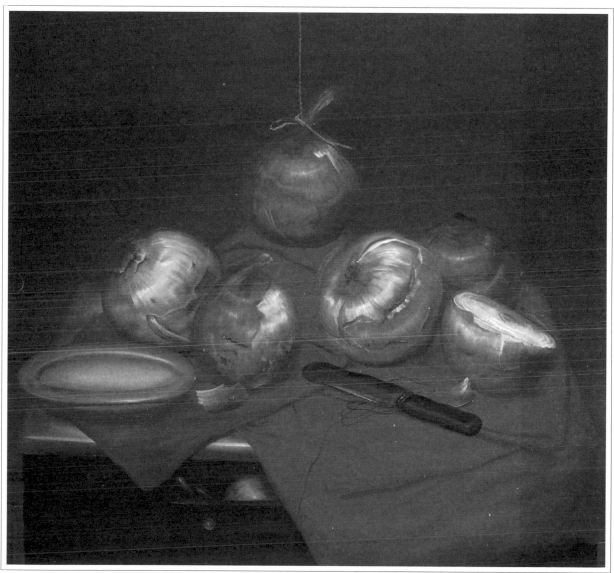

Fernando Botero, *Onions* (1974)

VEGETABLES

Artichokes à la Barigoule

Henri Deluy

ARTICHOKE: a specimen bristling with sharp spikes, its tips are often garnished. But also the "edible plant" that we know. For our artichoke is a thistle. A cultivated thistle, our vegetable is nothing other than the "capitulum of the plant before it blooms." It is the edible "receptacle," with a base of "bracts," our leaves. The name comes to us from the Arabic "al-kar-chouf," through the Spanish "alcarchofa," then "alcachofera," and from the Northern Italian "articiolo," itself an deformation of "carciofs." Well yes! It's full of choke (the unblossomed flowers), grows everywhere, likes the heat, and deep, loose ground; it's got long roots, multiplies by seeds or eye buds, and gets hard too fast; there are too many of them, they say (each year tons and tons are burned), and they're bitter: but don't let that stop you from enjoying them. Especially now that the new little ones have been here for a few weeks; we first ate them raw, with a vinaigrette sauce, in a salad, steamed, with little onions (see Jeannette Tortel's recipe in no. 96/97 of our journal)... We're going to try them *à la Barigoule* (*barigoulo,* "mushroom," in Provençal).

Take some purple artichokes, not macaus, if possible, wash them, trim them (remove the first row of leaves, cut the tips of the others, take out the choke). Put in a small saucepan, leaf side down, in which an onion, a handful of chopped shallots, and one or two carrots cut into thin strips are browning in olive oil. Season. Cover. Leave on the stove for 5 to 10 minutes, stirring. When they begin to turn brown, take them off the heat. Place the artichokes on a plate. Strain the sauce, throw out the oil. Put the casserole back on the stove with fresh oil, just a bit, and the artichokes, which you will have already filled with the following stuffing: *petit salé* ("half-salted, non-smoked pork belly"), what's left of the sauce that just browned (onion, shallot, etc.), another onion, another small handful of shallots, mushrooms, salt, coarse pepper, garlic, a pinch of nutmeg, parsley, all well chopped and lightly browned. Baste with a little broth, add one or two egg yolks. Let the stuffing cool. Garnish the artichokes. Place them, bottom down, in the hot saucepan, baste with two glasses of white wine, a little water, and one or two cloves of garlic. Cover with thin slices of bacon topped with a laurel and a thyme leaf. Cook gently, covered. Before serving, remove the bacon and add a dash of lemon.

Serve after fish. With the same wine. And the same appetite. With the sun and some friends.

N.B. If you can't find any purple artichokes, if you only have the common artichoke, blanch it for 5 to 10 minutes according to size, before proceeding with the recipe.

Translated by Guy Bennett

Spinach Gratin with Sardines

HENRI DELUY

GRATIN, the word is very old: from the XVIth Century. It "is descended from" the Germanic *kratton,* through the Old Provençal *gratar.* Originally, it meant that which remains at the bottom of a dish, or on one of its sides, and which can only be removed by scraping. In the particular meaning that we give it, it only goes back to the XIXth Century.

Spinach, with its branches, comes to us from Spain where, they say, it was brought by the Arabs. Likewise, the word *épinard* ["spinach"] has made the rounds: it comes from Persian through Medieval Latin and Old Provençal (where it got its "r"). Our language adopts it in 1331. It is found in nearly all the European languages. Spinach exists today in numerous garden varieties.

Our laziness—to put it bluntly—often keeps it from our tables for it takes a large quantity of spinach to make a dish and you have to clean and wash them… Still, it is a flavorful herb, as delicious raw, still young, in a salad as it is cooked,
accompanied by or, indeed *en gratin* with sardines (as for them, they took a Latin name meaning, literally, what was undoubtedly the privileged fishing place at the time: Sardinia).

Here's the recipe that I propose:

Use an earthenware casserole for the oven. Choose spinach sold with their roots. Prepare them well. Blanch them with a pinch of salt, a tiny pepper, a piece of fennel. Strain. Chop. Brown them in olive oil, in a frying pan, with one or two cloves of crushed garlic. Put the first layer of spinach in the oiled casserole. On top, put raw sardines, very fresh, very firm, without heads, scales or bones. Another layer of spinach, more rows of sardines. A little oil on top. No bread-crumbs. Cook it slowly in the oven. Serve when the top forms a light crust.

A simple edifice for a refinement of the pleasure of the palate.

Translated by Guy Bennett

Entrées

Djuna Barnes, *Pot-au-feu* (ca. 1930)

I

PASTA, PAELLA AND FISH

Spaghettini alla Bolognese

Pasta with Meat Sauce
For Four

RON PADGETT

INGREDIENTS

1 tablespoon olive oil

1 medium-sized onion

1 large clove of garlic

1 pound ground sirloin

Two pounds of fresh tomatoes (or a 28-ounce can of crushed tomatoes)

½ teaspoon salt

¼ teaspoon thyme

2 tablespoons basil

Water

(Optional: a carrot or two)

1 pound pasta

5–10 sprigs of fresh parsley, chopped fine

Grated cheese

Pepper

THE SAUCE

1. Put olive oil in a 9-inch frying pan.
2. Dice the onion and garlic and brown them in the pan over a medium flame.
3. Add ground sirloin. Keep breaking it up with, say, a wooden spoon, until it's all crumbly. The browner it gets, the easier it is to make it crumbly.
4. Add the tomatoes, cut up. (Don't worry, they'll cook down. You could substitute canned tomatoes, crushed or whole, and you could use a mixture of fresh tomatoes and crushed, but don't use tomato paste.)
5. When the meat is brown, add salt, thyme, and basil.
6. If the juice from the tomatoes doesn't cover the mixture, add enough water to cover.
7. (Optional: Add a chopped carrot or two.)
8. Reduce flame to a simmering low, and cover.
9. Cook for at least half an hour. Anytime the sauce starts to look heavy, like thick, boiling mud, stir in a little water.

THE PASTA

Any type is O.K. My favorite is spaghettini, or thin spaghetti, made of Italian semolina wheat. Don't use domestic pasta made only of softer wheat: it loses its character too easily.

1. Put 3 or 4 teaspoons of salt in a big pot of water, and bring to a violent boil.
2. Add 1 pound of pasta.
3. Cook to taste. I like spaghetti firm, noodles softer.

SERVING

1. Drain pasta and fork it into bowls. Add sauce. Top with fresh chopped parsley and a spoon or two of grated cheese, Romano or Parmesan (or, if you want, a healthy dollop of ricotta). Serve steaming hot. Don't stand around thinking about Yeats.

2. Let everyone add salt and pepper to taste.

MISCELLANEOUS REMARKS

1. This dish can be served as a first course, as in Italy, or, in larger helpings, as a main course.

2. You might want to serve it with a good loaf of bread, a green salad and/or green vegetable, fresh fruit, dessert, red wine, and water.

3. The unused sauce keeps well in the refrigerator, and heats up nicely. You can then extend it by adding tomatoes.

4. The amounts of ingredients above are approximate; sometimes I use more or less. Also, the ingredients themselves can be varied somewhat; you might want to leave out the garlic, and add celery or black olives. But don't use cheap hamburger, and if you insist on using tomato paste, add a little sugar to help offset the paste's acidity and hideous metallic taste. The aim is to make a sauce you'll enjoy eating without fear of any 3 A.M. aftereffects, a dish that's substantial but light.

Macaroni & Meat Pies

GIUSEPPE DI LAMPEDUSA

THE PRINCE was too experienced to offer Sicilian guests, in a town of the interior, a dinner beginning with soup, and he infringed the rules of *haute cuisine* all the more readily as he disliked it himself. But rumors of the barbaric foreign usage of serving insipid liquid as first course had reached the major citizens of Donnafugata too insistently for them not to quiver with a slight residue of alarm at the start of a solemn dinner like this. So when three lackeys in green, gold, and powder entered, each holding a great silver dish containing a towering mound of macaroni, only four of the twenty at table avoided showing their pleased surprise: the Prince and Princess from foreknowledge, Angelica from affectation, and Concetta from lack of appetite. All the others, including Tancredi, showed their relief in varying ways, from the fluty and ecstatic grunts of the notary to the sharp squeak of Francesco Paolo. But a threatening circular stare from the host soon stifled these improper demonstrations.

Good manners apart, though, the appearance of those monumental dishes of macaroni was worthy of the quivers of admiration they evoked. The burnished gold of the crusts, the fragrance of sugar and cinnamon they exuded, were but preludes to the delights released from the interior when the knife broke the crust; first came a mist laden with aromas, then chicken livers, hard-boiled eggs, sliced ham, chicken, and truffles in masses of piping-hot, glistening macaroni, to which the meat juice gave an exquisite hue of suède.

The beginning of the meal, as happens in the provinces, was quiet. The Archpriest made the sign of the Cross, and plunged in head-first without a word. The organist absorbed the succulent dish with closed eyes; he was grateful to the Creator that his ability to shoot hare and woodcock could bring him ecstatic pleasures like this, and the thought came to him that he and Teresina could exist for a month on the cost of one of these dishes. Angelica, the lovely Angelica, forgot her Tuscan affectations and part of her good manners and devoured her food with the appetite of her seventeen years and the vigor derived from grasping her fork halfway up the handle. Tancredi, in an attempt to link gallantry and greed, tried to imagine himself tasting, in the aromatic forkfuls, the kisses of his neighbor Angelica, but he realized at once that the experiment was disgusting and suspended it, with a mental reservation about reviving this fantasy with the pudding. The Prince, although rapt in the contemplation of Angelica sitting opposite him, was the only one able to note that the *demi-glace* was too rich, and made a mental note to tell the cook so next day; the others ate without thinking of anything, and without realizing that the food seemed so delicious because a whiff of sensuality had wafted into the house.

Translated by Archibald Colquhoun

Paella

Felipe Alfau

LEANING AGAINST the kitchen door, glass in hand and an eye on the proceedings, was Bejarano. Inside was Lunarito doing something at the kitchen table and in a corner, sitting in a chair with her arms folded, was the old lady Doña Felisa. The woman practically lived in the kitchen and only left the place to go to bed. No one had ever presented her to anyone and she scarcely spoke at all but sat there looking at everything with resigned understanding and a smile reminiscent of the Mona Lisa.

Bejarano greeted us and stepped aside, pushing us hospitably into the kitchen. The Moor said: "Not late for dinner, I hope." This was another aspect of the Bejarano ménage: anyone could arrive at dinnertime and bring whomever he pleased without previous invitation. The Moor continued:

"Paella again, I bet. From the looks of things and from past experience: paella."

"Yes, paella again," came with lugubrious patience from Doña Felisa.

"So it is paella again," Lunarito said, "and you seem to like it well enough. Don't you want to eat it, Moor? It will save me trouble. I won't have to make more."

"Oh, to be sure. In fact, I will prepare it myself inasmuch as I and my friends are going to eat it. That will save you more trouble. Let me see what you have here. If I am going to eat it again, I am going to have it cooked right."

This precipitated a violent argument between Lunarito and the Moor, Lunarito swearing that she would not lift a finger and he could do everything by himself, including the unpleasant attending chores of washing and peeling this and that. Meanwhile Bejarano was pouring drinks for everybody, including a surprisingly tall one for Doña Felisa. Don Pedro recoiled from his:

"Not that. I am not going to drink that at this time of day and before dinner. You are supposed to be so castizo and you drink that thing! A true Spaniard never drinks anything Spanish before meals. He drinks Italian vermouth. You have some Cinzano there, I know. Bring it out but use the same kind of glass, big."

"There is some lemon there too," put in Lunarito, "although I don't see why I should bother with you."

"No. No lemon. Only plain and in a big glass." He got what he wanted and went straight to the refrigerator. He placed his shillelagh on the nearby table and then brought out two chickens and laid them on the table. He began to squeeze and poke them with expert fingers: "Hmmm—they could be more tender, but they'll do. The technique of the old maestro will tame them. You know." He reminisced about those people in Spain who grow chickens for eggs on roofs. When one of the chickens won't lay or is slow, they hold it over a bed and squeeze for all they are worth. He pantomimed while talking:

"Come on there, you lazy chicken, let go of that egg—These Spaniards are inimitable and most of the time they get their egg." He addressed Lunarito: "I am going to cut up and clean these chickens. You get the olives and rice and fix more peppers and chop a lot more garlic, and don't go foreign and independent on me. You and your pressure cooker for the chickens—it is formidable. They could sell all of them in Spain, but not for cooking but to press the eggs out of the lazy chickens—The National System, always use everything for what it is not intended. Put the pressure cooker away. I cook this in the black iron casseroles, although a paella should be cooked in a paella. Where are the casseroles?" He found them under the stove. "There seem to be enough chorizos," he mused to himself.

"Better put in more chorizos," chimed in Bejarano. "I like them and I am hungry."

"More chorizos it is," sighed the Moor. With remarkable speed, no doubt born from long experience, he was cutting chorizos in slices and dissecting chickens like a surgeon. Lunarito, her argument forgotten, had obediently done as ordered and brought all the ingredients. Don Pedro picked up the bottle of olive oil:

"This is Italian, but no matter; just as good." He interrupted himself with a start: "Where are the clams and the shrimps?"

"The clams are right there in front of you and here are the shrimps." Lunarito brought a bowl of shrimps from the refrigerator.

"These are the clams? In these jars? All shelled? Have you lost the last vestige of mind you had left?"

"I like them that way. One gets all clams and not shells mixed up with the rice and taking up room, and while we are about it, that's why I like the pressure cooker; one can cook a chicken in it so that the bones come out easily and then one does not have bones taking up room and…"

"All right, all right. You win." He lifted his shoulders and then let them drop with a deep sigh: "I still say a paella should be cooked in a paella, but…this is what things have come to. Paella Newyorkina— I tell you, these Spaniards—" He took a good swallow of his vermouth: "I need the stimulant, but as I was saying: they were living in Spain, in primitive bliss, with those things which could not possibly be improved because they were born perfect, and when they leave Spain, they begin to think. They try to simplify and that's when the complications begin because they lose track of the original plan. It's hopeless. They join all the foreigners in that absolute incapacity to understand the obvious, they become reasonable, traitors and forsaken by God."

"Such sanctimonious words coming from the Moor." It was Dr. de los Rios standing at the kitchen door: "Don't let me interrupt while you are in such a mood."

"The Dr. Jesucristo," Don Pedro cried, "to my arms." He limped over with arms outstretched and then stopped. "I can't. My hands are all messed up, but christen your gullet and watch me do what I can with what I have. You, Lunarito, put some of the juice from those accursed clams in some container and soak some saffron in it." He limped back to the stove, poured the oil in the casseroles, and then in went the garlic, the pieces of chicken, and the seasoning. He kept a running commentary: "We'll give it a little more time, to tame the chickens," then he eyed the large refrigerator with disgust:

"That ridiculous white elephant. Like the pressure cooker, it is only a domestic example of the second law of thermodynamics. In one, time passes fast; in the other, slow. No wonder people live in such confusion. The old-fashioned cool room was much better. Food developed more flavor, you know?" He chuckled to himself. "It reminds me of an extraordinary business venture on which the Chink was going to embark." He always referred to the Señor Olózaga as the Chink. "We baptized it the Case of the Vanishing Refrigerator—that Chink! Simply no one like him. You know how things are here about advertising all these gadgets. Lunarito and Bejarano here have been long enough in this country to learn only the bad things."

His head nodded toward the clams: "But you know about this advertising pressure—your pressure cooker, Lunarito, that's good, double advertising pressure. Get the eggs out of your chickens faster—but you don't know what it's all about anyway. The Chink learns fast, even if his materialism is purely illusory. This was a fitting counterpart for his other inspiration of selling the sand in the Sahara Desert as a cleanser and at the same time forming an international combine to fill in the space with water and make a sea out of it. A great idealist, but this time it was the refrigerator. You must remember how some enterprising manufacturer discovered that when a solicitous housewife approaches her refrigerator with both hands occupied, she cannot open the door. So, he thought up a pedal that would do exactly this. However, this had the drawback that some people might lose their balance and fall, breaking dishes, hurting themselves, and then, you know? They have all learned about suing in court—the International System, of course. Well, the Chink thought up a better one. Have a refrigerator without a door and maintain a lower temperature. See the connection? One can see what's inside without opening the door, use more electricity, obtain a commission from the electric companies, and at the same time save in the manufacture of doors. Beautiful, I tell you; a nonexistent source of profit and a good selling point at the same time. Oh! The combinatory powers of the Chink. But having conceived this, he went further; there was no stopping him now. He said to himself: Why a refrigerator at all? Why not market a nonexistent refrigerator? Step by step, the refrigerator has vanished—an irresistible selling point, and the profits, immense. One can lower the price considerably, claiming that the space saved in shipping this nonexistent refrigerator, as well as the savings in manufacture, are being passed on to the consumer and competition is smashed. Besides, it has the undeniable advantage of taking no room at all in the kitchens of the consumers. No doors to open, no fatal falls, no lawsuits. But besides, in the space left by this refrigerator, one can install one of those, by that time, wonderfully fashionable old-fashioned oaken iceboxes purchased at some auction upstate with the savings from the vanishing refrigerator. Masterfully rounded, eh? That Chink—but I suppose that by now he has forgotten all about it, like he did about the Sahara Desert. His is a love for the business itself. Once conceived, once planned and solved, he loses interest. He wants the general solution. The numerical solution is for the lesser mortals who must be shown. His business ventures have been refined until they vanish like his refrigerator."

By this time, Don Pedro decided that the chickens were cooked enough. He called for the rest of the things, cooked the peppers a while, poured in the rice, the shrimps, pitted olives, and finally gave in and shook the clams out of the jars and onto the whole thing. Then he doused in the saffronized clam juice, added more water ostentatiously without measuring it and with an air that said, "That's only for beginners." Then with a grand swipe of his hand he turned the burner on full blast.

As he washed his hands under the tap, his whole back consoled: "Just a little more patience, my children. I have done my best to feed you and after all, my best   " He picked up his shillelagh from the table, once more the conductor, and we moved to the dining room. As we crossed the door he shot over his shoulder: "When the water boils, cover the pots and turn the fire very low. You can take care of the rest, I trust, Lunarito." He kept going without seeing the murderous look of Lunarito.

Joseph Cornell, *A Pantry Ballet for Jacques Offenbach* (1942)
[dancing lobsters]

PASTA, PAELLA AND FISH

Oyster Stew & Vodka

ALAIN BOSQUET

ONE GLOOMY NIGHT of November, 1957, in a wooden house on Cape Cod, Conrad Aiken was treating me to one of my most memorable meals. The mist was heavy, and the waves were slapping the stones at regular intervals. We were comparing the merits of several brands of vodka, then quite an un-American drink. Conrad preferred the straight Russian brand, whereas my preference went to the Polish taste of the drink that reminded me of several flavors mixed together. Neither one of us had sympathy for Canadian vodka, and we hadn't discovered then the delights of the Finnish version. Conrad brought a sort of bucket full of dozens of oysters in what he called a soup and which was only a gallon of very hot milk mixed with cream. It was sizzling hot, and I soon discovered that oysters were of two kinds: the flat, green species and also the fatter type with an ivory hue. On the bottom of the bucket there were layers of several herbs that gave a particular taste to the dish; dill, tarragon and especially chives. As I filled my large and deep plate, he reached an arm across the fumes and poured some old brandy in it. We then discussed the contents of the bucket, and I realized he had added smoked clams and, probably to amaze me, one or two seahorses, the recipe of which he must have learned from the numerous Chinese cookbooks he had read in his youth. These poor little creatures tasted like very dull dried shrimps. Soon he replaced the brandy with two or three spoonfuls of French cognac, which enabled us again to compare the merits of Rémy Martin, Martell and Hine. Needless to say, when we were about to fill our plates for the third time our spirits were quite high, so we talked about the poets we loved. It appeared we had a common admiration for Emily Dickinson and Hart Crane, whereas we had misgivings about T.S. Eliot and even Walt Whitman. When we felt we were getting quite drunk indeed, we embraced and shouted: "Death to Lord Tennyson!" Conrad, whose nose had become quite violet, indigo and mauve, quoted Li Po. I could not contend with his knowledge of Chinese philosophers and misquoted a few. I even believe that I invented one or two aphorisms. Conrad's look was suspicious, but the meal went on until we stopped hearing the tempest outside. The next morning, after all the hot coffee, English muffins and medlar marmalade, we serenely spoke of prose writers. Being both poets, we were quite severe with Stendhal, Dickens, Tolstoy and other competitors.

Two Large Fish In Jelly

BRUNO SCHULZ

THOSE WEEKS passed under the sign of a strange drowsiness.

Beds unmade for days on end, piled high with bedding crumpled and disordered from the weight of dreams, stood like deep boats waiting to sail into the dank and confusing labyrinths of some dark starless Venice. In the bleakness of dawn, Adela brought us coffee. Lazily we started dressing in the cold rooms, in the light of a single candle reflected many times in black window panes. The mornings were full of aimless bustle, of prolonged searches in endless drawers and cupboards. The clacking of Adela's slippers could be heard all over the flat. The shop assistants lit the lanterns, took the large shop keys which mother handed them and went out into the thick swirling darkness. Mother could not come to terms with her dressing. The candles burnt smaller in the candlesticks. Adela disappeared somewhere into the furthest rooms or into the attic where she hung the washing. She was deaf to our calling. A newly lit, dirty, bleak fire in the stove licked at the cold, shiny growth of soot in the throat of the chimney. The candle died out, and the room filled with gloom. With our heads on the tablecloth, among the remains of breakfast, we fell asleep, still half-dressed. Lying face downward on the furry lap of darkness, we sailed in its regular breathing into the starless nothingness. We were awakened by Adela's noisy tidying up. Mother could not cope with her dressing. Before she had finished doing her hair, the shop-assistants were back for lunch. The half-light in the market place was now the colour of golden smoke. For a moment it looked as if out of that smoke-coloured honey, that opaque amber, a most beautiful afternoon would unfold. But the happy moment passed, the amalgam of dawn withered, the swelling fermentation of the day, almost completed, receded again into a helpless greyness. We assembled again around the table, the shop assistants rubbed their hands, red from the cold, and the prose of their conversation suddenly revealed a fullgrown day, a grey and empty Tuesday, a day without tradition and without a face. But it was only when a dish appeared on the table containing two large fish in jelly lying side by side, head to tail, like a sign of the Zodiac, that we recognised in them the coat of arms of that day the calendar emblem of the nameless Tuesday: we shared it out quickly among ourselves, thankful that the day had at last achieved an identity.

The shop assistants ate with unction, with the seriousness due to a calendar feast. The smell of pepper filled the room. And when they had used pieces of bread to wipe up the remains of the jelly from their plates, pondering in silence on the heraldry of the following days of the week, and nothing remained on the serving dish but the fishheads with their boiled out eyes, we all felt that by a communal effort we had conquered the day and that what remained of it did not matter.

Translated by Celina Wieniewska

The Salmon is Always Underdone

VIRGINIA WOOLF

THE PRIME MINISTER was coming, Agnes said: so she had heard them say in the dining-room, she said, coming in with a tray of glasses. Did it matter, did it matter in the least, one Prime Minister more or less? It made no difference at this hour of the night to Mrs. Walker among the plates, saucepans, cullenders, frying-pans, chicken in aspic, ice-cream freezers, pared crusts of bread, lemons, soup tureens, and pudding basins which, however hard they washed up in the scullery seemed to be all on top of her, on the kitchen table, on chairs, while the fire blared and roared, the electric lights glared, and still supper had to be laid. All she felt was, one Prime Minister more or less made not a scrap of difference to Mrs. Walker.

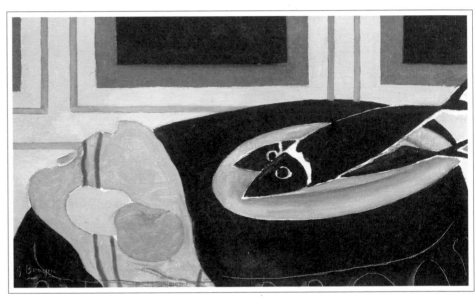
Georges Braque, *Blackfish* (1942)

The ladies were going upstairs already, said Lucy; the ladies were going up, one by one, Mrs. Dalloway walking last and almost always sending back some message to the kitchen, "My love to Mrs. Walker," that was it one night. Next morning they would go over the dishes—the soup, the salmon; the salmon, Mrs. Walker knew, as usual underdone, for she always got nervous about the pudding and left it to Jenny; so it happened, the salmon was always underdone. But some lady with fair hair and silver ornaments had said, Lucy said, about the entrée, was it really made at home? But it was the salmon that bothered Mrs. Walker, as she spun the plates round and round, and pulled in dampers and pulled out dampers; and there came a burst of laughter from the dining-room; a voice speaking; then another burst of laughter—the gentlemen enjoying themselves when the ladies had gone. The tokay, said Lucy running in. Mr. Dalloway had sent for the tokay, from the Emperor's cellars, the Imperial Tokay.

Jhabvala's Fish Pilao

for 4:

RUTH PRAWER JHABVALA

1 ½ lb filets of any firm-fleshed fish

½ cup yogurt

2 cups rice

3 cups stock or water

4 tablespoons vegetable oil

2 medium-sized onions, finely chopped

2 medium-sized tomatoes, finely chopped

1" ginger root, peeled and chopped fine

1 teaspoon turmeric

1 teaspoon ground coriander

½ teaspoon caraway or poppy seeds

12 cloves

8 peppercorns

1" stick cinnamon

1 green chili, sliced (optional)

Cut fish into bite-size pieces. Sprinkle with salt and black pepper and cover with the yogurt. Marinate for half an hour.

Fry onions in the oil, and just before they turn brown, add ginger, cloves, turmeric, peppercorns, cinnamon, chili, coriander, caraway or poppy seeds, and chopped tomatoes. Fry for 3 minutes. Add rice and fry for 1 minute. Add stock or water and 1 teaspoon salt and bring to boil. Lower flame and tightly cover pan. Remove fish from marinade with a slotted spoon. In separate pan fry fish till lightly golden. Just before all the liquid evaporates from the rice—about 10 minutes—add fried fish and mix in with the rice. Put lid on tightly and turn flame up for 2 minutes. Then turn flame off and let the mixture cook in steam for 10 minutes.

Sprinkle rice with chopped parsley or fresh coriander and garnish with slices of hardboiled egg. Serve with lentils (*dal*) and cucumber grated in yogurt (*raita*)—for both these recipes see *Ismail Merchant's Indian Cuisine* (St. Martin's Press, 1986).

II

STEWS, GAMEBIRDS, RABBIT

Suppah! Suppah!

G. V. Desani

ALL HASTILY put on their shoes!

The better-caste cooks bolt from the back door.

Not a word of thanks or apology is said.

I turn to Banerrji with a quick appealing look.

"Mr H. Hatterr," he says it first, and with an unmistakable note of dejection, "in your home, poets have been insulted! O my God!"

As I am unable to accompany Banerrji, being in the seminude, I am loitering in the garden, the hearth's borderline, seeking shelter from the sheriff within *and* the downpour without!

The rain continues to rain like hell!

In the interim…

I see my servantwallahs returning emotionally-fortified from the movie meller-drammer!

Both of 'em deliberately ignore me, under my own personal parasol, passing on, verbum sap!

Having thus maltreated the master of the house—had a dam' good time on his money, used his umbrella without permit— inside, they are making a devil of a fuss over née Rialto.

She has the furniture brought in, while I am looking on, sheltering in the yonder cow-shed: the neighbours being safe home: guffawing, actually in stitches…

And I hear impatient orders for supper: *suppah! suppah!*

Damme, a cosy tête-à-tête with Appadine-Sinclair, and the Lydia woman, while her wedded is flung out of the house!

And the lista de platos offered—on the house!—includes such par excellence stuff as fried saffron rice, *kofta* meat balls browned with garlic and spice, Bengali kebab-goulash with mango and lime chutnee, pickles pampered in mustard oil, the sweet course fried by *my* fellers, and coffee *garam*-hot! No. 1 chow for all *but* her own benedict and goodman!

Meanwhile, I take my turn at the french windows, watching these hospitality proceedings—and having my back washed, the Devil's spits! raining and blowing, relentlessly.

After the happening, I lost face a posteriori.

Damme, having been made a laughing stock in my own house and neighbourhood, and having had my guests nearly machine-gunned, I couldn't very well show off!

Shikar Korma or Honeybraised Pork

ROSMARIE WALDROP

2 lb. cubed pork
2 T honey
4 T butter
1 bunch scallions
1 clove garlic
½ tsp turmeric

½–1 cup yogurt
some orange and lemon peel
pinch of cardamom
½ tsp cinnamon
¼ tsp mace
½ tsp pepper
salt

Heat the honey and butter in a heavy-bottomed saucepan. Brown the cubed pork in it on high heat. (One layer of meat at a time). When all the pork is browned combine it with the yogurt, chopped scallions and garlic, orange & lemon peel, spices, and simmer for c. 45 minutes. The yogurt and spices should form a thick sauce. I usually take the lid off during the latter part of the simmering so that it won't be too liquid.

I once served this to Jack Hawkes who went wild over the "golden globules" and then came out with: "You know what it reminds me of is horse manure!" I *think* the similarity was shape rather than taste, but I never found out for sure.

Plov

ARKADII DRAGOMOSCHENKO

serves 10 persons

Inevitably I forgot one thing when we talked over the phone yesterday: Arkadii dictated to me a recipe for your book. I give it to you in its Soviet form, in kilograms, with instructions assuming Soviet ingredients—oil capable of two smokes and rice amenable to an hour's soaking followed by two hours of cooking. We tested the recipe in Michael Davidson's kitchen in San Diego. The second smoke set off the smoke alarm. And the rice was gummy where it should properly be firm, with each grain separate. We were using long grain white rice. The long grain is important, and I think perhaps Basmati rice would be best, with no prior soaking, and added much later in the cooking.

—LYN HEJINIAN

1 kilogram strong, long grain white rice
1 kilogram lamb, cubed
260 grams cottonseed or sunflower oil
1 kilogram carrots, chopped
½ kilogram onion, chopped
½ to 1 teaspoon cayenne pepper
a handful of sour dried apricots, chopped
2 teaspoons basil or garam masala, depending on preference
sour pickles, chopped
fresh parsley, finely chopped
fresh dill, finely chopped
scallions, chopped
6 or 7 whole cloves of garlic

Soak the dried apricots in unsalted water for one hour.
Soak the rice for one hour in salted water.

To prepare the *zirvak*: heat the oil over very high flame, waiting for the second smoke; the first smoke is gray, the second will be blue. At the blue smoke, add one small piece each of carrot and onion and allow them to blacken for 30 seconds; then discard them. This will remove impurities from the oil. Add the lamb, turning it until the surface is pink, just on the verge of browning. Lower heat to medium and add the chopped onion and carrots; cook, stirring frequently, for 20 minutes. Add ½ to 1 tsp. cayenne pepper and 1 tsp. salt. After 10 minutes add hot water to the depth of two fingers (approx. 3 centimeters), turn heat down to very low, and simmer for 40 minutes. Add more water if the *zirvak* begins to get dry.

After 40 minutes add 2 tsps. of either garam masala or of dry basil; oregano might be used in place of either, also. Add a handful of soaked, dried apricots. Simmer for 5 minutes.

Now slowly add the soaked rice with a large spoon to the *zirvak*. Add hot water to 3 centimeters above level of rice and simmer for 1 or 1 ½ hours. Taste the rice from time to time—if the top layer is dry, add a little water and poke a few holes in the surface to allow steam to rise.

When the rice is close to done, insert whole cloves of garlic deep into the *plov*.

To serve: On a large serving platter sprinkle a layer of chopped greens (pickle, parsley, dill, and scallions). Then add the layer of rice, another layer of greens, and then mound the *zirvak* over the rice and cover with a final layer of greens.

This recipe is based on Soviet ingredients. Our white rice is very strong and American rice is much less so. The rice in the *plov* should not be gummy; the grains should be separate and firm. If you are using American rice, omit the soaking and cook the rice for a shorter amount of time.

In the South they add raisins to the *plov* along with the apricots, but in my opinion this makes the dish too sweet. The dish should hover between sweet and sour tastes.

With the *plov* you must drink straight vodka.

That's all. If it's not perfect the first time, don't despair. And if you achieve great results, write to me please; I will be proud to share your success.

Translated by Lyn Hejinian

Pot au Loup (Wolfish Pot)

MAC WELLMAN

FILL a five-quart earthenware pot with the following: two or three large onions, sliced; two medium-sized turnips or large parsnips; approximately half a red cabbage in inch-thick slices; a large carrot peeled and sliced; and several potatoes, ditto. Upon this elegant bed of vegetable wholesomeness place, with love, three to four pounds of fresh breast of veal, sliced between each rib to make four or five servings. This should pretty much fill the pot, but there should be sufficient room still for approximately twenty to thirty garlic cloves, in their shells (baked at high temperature garlic loses its bitterness, and becomes a delectable buttery paste). Sprinkle the completed pot with fresh rosemary and fresh-ground pepper.

Cover the pot and place in an oven pre-heated to 425 degrees. Bake for an hour and a half, then turn off the oven. After an additional half hour, remove from oven and serve.

Wolfish pot, like love, is better the next day, and the clear veal and vegetable broth remaining makes a fine soup stock (see Wolfish Soup). The meal is ideal for cold, dark, Wolfish winter nights before or after fits of howling.

Bigos

PIOTR SZEWC

ENTERING THE TAVERN, Walek stumbled on a straw doormat and the whole place spun before his eyes. The doormat was frayed and creased, soaked with melted snow. The sour smell of fermenting wine, of beer tapped from the barrels, of vodka, and the nauseating smell of warmed-up bodies, sheepskin coats, leftover food—all those smells placed Walek in the world which he had watched through the little hole scratched in the windowpane. It was a world that he couldn't quite imagine.

Grandfather ordered a plate of sauerkraut stew ("Make sure the *bigos* is hot"). When Walek swallowed a few heaping spoonfuls, he felt his blood quicken in his feet and hands, and he wiped sweat drops off his forehead. The chunks of venison in the stew tasted different—did they?—from the venison and *bigos* cooked by his old aunt, Jadwiga, who was in charge of the Danilowskis' kitchen. And he, Walek, will never forget—because there are things, events, people that must never be forgotten—the taste of *bigos* eaten with rye bread, the meat carelessly chewed, the quickly cleaned plate. And he won't forget—because this mustn't be forgotten either—the taste of the first beer that he drank sitting in his grandfather's lap. Encouraged by the laughter of the amused patrons, Walek got away with his audacity because Grandfather pretended not to see what Walek was doing. After a few days when Grandfather told Walek's mother about it, she was shocked. In the name of God and in the name of Walek's love for her, she begged her son never to drink beer if he didn't want to see her dead. Walek promised he would never touch beer without her knowledge and permission.

Translated by Ewa Hryniewicz-Yarbrough

Wiener Wurst Goulash

RAYMOND FEDERMAN

à la Erica Federman

¼ cup vegetable oil or shortening

6 large onions

2 cloves of garlic, mashed

2½ cups canned tomatoes, undrained

2 tablespoons paprika

salt & pepper to taste

2 pounds knockwurst sliced half-inch thick

3 large potatoes, peeled and quartered

optional: 2 carrots, sliced in half rounds; 1 green pepper, diced

1. In a large heavy pan heat oil and cook onions and garlic slowly until onions are golden, but not roasted. (Stir occasionally).
2. Add tomatoes, potatoes, optional vegetables, paprika and salt & pepper, cover and simmer until the potatoes are almost done (about 20 minutes).
3. Add the knockwurst, cover until the meat is thoroughly heated.

NOTE: This goulash is best when prepared ahead and allowed to rest overnight.

Serve with rye bread and a green salad (or cucumber salad).

Larks & Nightingales

JENS BJØRNEBOE

ALL: [*Turning enthusiastically to him*] Caruso!

CAVALLI: What have you got?

> CARUSO *takes some small birds out of his sack. He drinks from a glass on the bar, through the following.*

FIDELE: Two larks. Three nightingales.

PICCOLINO: Chestnuts, sherry sauce, truffles and cognac. Black olives. Mushrooms.

FIDELE: Garlic for the nightingale. That's how Grandma did it.

MARCO: Sage, bacon, chicken liver and Marsala.

SANDRO: I only said that I like those fat girls. Is there something wrong in that also? What?! !

MARCO: The bird lovers will stop us, Caruso.

CAVALLI: Caruso doesn't like bird lovers. He's biased.

MARCO: It is not everyone who has been executed and afterwards has risen from the dead. That was in the town of Bonzo.

CARUSO: Twenty years ago Father Piccolino raised me from the dead. That is his only miracle.

CAVALLI: Since Caruso was shot he can't stand bird fanciers. He has become a bigot.

Translated by Frederick Wasser

Thrush on Sliced Bread

HENRI DELUY

IT PROVIDES a beautiful page to Mme de Sévigné, another to Linné, yet another to Jules Renard, for it gave us two of the most simple, popular, and frequently used proverbs in the French language: *soûl comme une grive* [lit.: "drunk as a thrush," i.e. "drunk as a skunk"], *faute de grives on mange des merles* [lit.: "for lack of thrushes we're eating blackbirds," i.e., "beggars can't be choosers"], and its story is linked to that of the vineyard and the grape harvests in which, in its own way, it loves to participate. The word is found as early as the 13th Century; it makes allusion, in its etymology, to the migrations of this elegant, slender bird of average size, with russet, gray, and slate feathers, and whose stomach, lighter in color, is speckled with white patches. The thrush, which sings (they say that it twitters), is divided into about twenty species; the typical species is the "missel thrush" (or "great thrush," or "high thrush," or "large thrush") but, in restaurants, the most frequently served is the "fieldfare" or vine thrush, called common thrush, which is a little smaller and more appropriate for a single portion. In the Alps, and in Provence where many of them gorge themselves on juniper berries, you find the "sha-sha," a bit plump, favored by gluttons because there's more to eat, and the *quine*, which is finer and more savory. That's the one we'll choose. It must be rather young, with tight feathers. You keep it in a cool place for seven to eight days so that it's slightly gamy (much less than the woodcock), hung just long enough to tenderize the flesh and glorify the aroma. Don't gut it.

For the meal: pluck it well, singe it, bard it with slices of bacon (not too thick), salt it, put it on the spit in your oven, high heat for 8 to 10 minutes; broad slices of bread, at least two per thrush, are placed beneath to catch the juice and drippings. To serve (after a light but highly flavorful entrée to prepare the mouth for the violence of the game): hot plates, slices of bread on the bottom. Every one cuts open his *quine* on the bread and spreads it out, then you can attack the thrush, having tasted the toasted bread. Balance in passion. With a congenial wine: a *gigondas* for example.

Translated by Guy Bennett

Partridges with Small Vegetables

HENRI DELUY

THE *perdreau* and the *perdrix* ["partridges"], are both one and the same thing, and not at all alike. They are not the male and the female (the cock is called a *garron,* from the Provençal *garroun*) the *perdreau* is a young *perdrix* of the year, which has not yet reached its adult weight, and whose flesh is tender, extremely flavorful. *A la Saint-Rémi, tous les perdreaux sont perdrix* ["By the Feast Day of Saint Rémi, all of the *perdreaux* are *perdrix*"], in the month of October all of the *perdreaux* are plump and large enough to be called *perdrix.* The best period for *perdreaux* is September. That's when the *perdreaux* companies are most interesting to us.

The bird and its choice meat were known to the Romans; it is from the Latin words *perdrix* and *gallus* (cock) that the 13th Century French *perdrigal* is born. *Perdrigal* becomes *perdrieau,* found in the 16th Century, then *perdreau.* Our *perdrix,* that's the generic name, is squat, without a crest; it has a short tail, exposed nostrils, and a short, thick beak. Numerous varieties are known. The gray partridge is prized by gourmets (and rightly so, in my opinion). The red-legged partridge is plumper—restaurateurs prefer this one, from which they get two portions. It is less savory. The rock partridge is also known, it's a sort of red-legged partridge that lives in the mountains, and is not inconsiderable; and the *francolin,* close to the partridge, but less delicate.

Partridges that live in uncovered regions and walk as often as they fly are monogamous in mating season. They are a fragile species; only the considerable number of eggs, from 9 to 17 per clutch, and hunting regulations assure its conservation. For our pleasure, as they make an exceptional meal.

For Autumn, the right season, I propose the following classic recipe. You need one *perdreau* per person, and two old *perdrix* (they are harder, but more sapid). You color your *perdrix* with a little lard in a large casserole dish. Remove the fat. Once again add a little lard to the *perdrix,* along with bacon rind, a cabbage heart (that you will have blanched beforehand), carrots, radishes, green beans, peas, mixed

René Magritte, *Pleasure* (1926)

herbs, and two cloves of garlic. Baste lightly. Braise them gently. In time, add a few potatoes. Also in time (about half an hour before serving) you roast your *perdreaux*— you have singed them quickly, you have trussed them and wrapped them with thin slices of bacon. You serve the *perdreaux*—I prefer them not too red—on a bed of the well-strained vegetables. The juice of the *perdreaux* is served on the side.

It is one of the first marvels of cooked nature.

P.S.: The old *perdrix* are kept in reserve. I don't throw them away: I remove the flesh with which I make a stuffing, with a hand of soft, white cheese, for rolls which go in the oven the following day.

Proverb: "To eat partridges without oranges": to be satisfied with a good thing, without adding any unnecessary refinements.

Translated by Guy Bennett

Sparrows

JOHN HAWKES

IN MY MOUTH the smoke was the color of mustard, around my ears the curling hair was both gold and gray, overhead the night was thick with stars. So I had no regrets. I smelled the peppery darkness, retrieved the pot and left it where Rosella could dump the snails down the hole in the flat stone of our crude lavatory in the morning. Then I groped my way toward Rosella and the light of the olive-twig fire, the smell of smoke.

At first glance I thought the crock was packed with fur, because by the uneven light of Rosella's fire the soft brown substance rising somewhat higher than the square mouth of the crock rippled and gleamed softly, was alight with richness and flashing colors so that it suggested fur. But my fingers told me immediately that the crock was packed not with fur but birds. I could feel their concealed bodies smaller than the bodies of mice, could feel the fiercely contracted wings, the feet like flecks of wire, the little beaks that made me think of the sharp nibs of old-fashioned pens. I seized one by a brittle wing and held it to the light and recognized it immediately as some kind of sparrow. More than three or four dozen sparrows in a stone crock, and obviously Rosella intended to cook them all. And weighing the almost weightless bird in my palm I knew, suddenly, that the crock was a gift and that all the time we were hunting snails Rosella had known it would arrive, was perhaps instrumental in its arrival.

Had she asked that disfigured youth to shoot sparrows among the rocks and in the steep, sparsely wooded hills near the sanctuary? On her demand had he spent all day discharging his untrustworthy weapon at those swift targets? Had Catherine heard those very shots? And was all this for me? All this for the idle middle-aged man from over the mountains? Three or four dozen sparrows, I thought, were a good many.

We cooked them together, ate them together. For the first time I not only ate with Rosella but joined her in that damp cavelike room of stone and tile where, until now, Rosella had moved alone with a young woman's bored carelessness through all her days and nights of cooking. I joined her and removed my black coat and in frayed shirt sleeves and soiled vest sat beside my standing Rosella and helped her, pulled the feathers from my share of the sparrows, which was no easy job, and despite my size hovered as near as I could to her shoulder while inside the casserole she built up the layers: butter, thyme, sparrows, onions, butter, thyme, sparrows, onions, and so forth. She prepared a sauce and I scrubbed out the iron vessel. Hovering stolidly beside Rosella, I sniffed the now browning sparrows and fed the fire, felt the oil of the cooking birds on my own brow and on my cheeks, felt without a single touch each movement of Rosella's small bones, muscles, ligaments. I watched Rosella's fingers at work, fingers even now stained with the black earth of my garden. Sometime toward the end of these preparations I sighed a deep sigh and realized that next time I too would be able to tie the wings, chop off the miniature feet.

"The heads. I see we eat the heads, Rosella. And the beaks. For the full effect we must eat the entire bird. I understand."

Her example was not at first easy to follow. Beaks that were very much like little split black fingernails. Heads smaller than my thumb and without eyes. I noticed such details, calmly watched how Rosella ate each sparrow in a single bite, and realized that it would be difficult for even a seasoned sex-aesthetician to follow her example. But then I saw that Rosella's two front teeth overlapped each other, and at this observation, this further instance of poignant incongruity, I could hesitate no more. And there amidst heat, shadows like finger puppets, savory taste and savory thoughts, how wrong I was to have hesitated in the first place. Because thanks to Rosella's cooking, the sparrows, I found, were simply soft and crunchy too, as if the different textures of sweetness had been so combined that it was still necessary to chew a moment that very substance which had in fact already dissolved, melted, in the aching mouth.

"Rosella," I said, with my jaws working and elbows propped casually on the table, "magnificent!"

How Rabbit & Hare Are Best Dealt With

PIERRE JORIS

NICOLE PEYRATITTE
& PIERRE JORIS,
EACH IN HIS/HER OWN WAY,
TELL OF HOW RABBIT & HARE
WAS & IS BEST DEALT WITH,
BOTH HERE
IN THE NEW WORLD
& BACK THERE
IN THE OLD.

for Diane & Jerry Rothenberg

"OUR RABBIT left thes" tentative scratchings in the top margin
who knows what this irregular plural of "the" points to
could be the propagational speeds the creature is known for
could be its many incarnational variations in darwinian
space its run at continental drift its strong zigzag back legs
jumping off points for tales of old o pulque aztec moon god
o coney island of our bellies o you the meat of whose fully developed
foetus was classified, like eggs, as 'no meat' by the church
in the middle ages thus letting monks eat you on fasting days
o but what did *this* rabbit leave or why not right
there & then gnawing itself through the top margin &
thus out of the picture of the menu though we will
not eat you that way always already *à la carte* whichever
one is dealt you the eater or the eaten an enn for an are
a hen for a hare in Nicole's pyrenean aspiration
in this our dare-winian alphabet soup
I eat you are eaten my bunny my rabbit my mother
used to call me "He'eschen" little hare that was in Europe
where at least one discrimination has survived the confusions
a rabbit is not a hare & vice-versa & on our nursery
walls Dürer's hare stared into space til the fox caught up
& the two real pet rabbits I left to starve in teenage forgetfulness a
karmic flaw bound to come back & haunt me in the form of
my next incarnation a wild hare darting through woods

til 100 hard huffing pellets of birdshot spin its

7 salto mortale's o little zigzag god of the impossible flight

o little god of zigzag handwriting like those tall hieratic egyptian

zoomorphs you too will be prepared for the long trip you will hang

for two days in a cool room in your coat a bardo thödol of slow

intestinal decomposition my mouth already waters

grandfather always said use only the very best bottle

of old burgundy at least 3 nights you will lie in it

o soused hare of my zigzag mind with your head

left on they now call you *huesenziwwi* & ceremoniously

count 3 shallots 1 carrot 3 cloves of garlic 1 parsley

root 1 sage leave some thyme laurel good olive oil black

pepper 3 or 4 cloves some tarragon into this marinade this

brine of the rest of your life for our delight

you will rest all night in the fridge next to the cup holds

your blood mixed with vinegar o zigzag jesus hare

you who are the worst uphill racer in zoomorphdom

& should have known better every few hours I turn your

limbs in the fragrant herbal wine & will try to forget my

little zigzag self in brine *me'in he'eschen* for three days

in the morgue of our appetites now bacon browns in a

cast iron pot in go your cold & soaked limbs brown

well a glass of armagnac at hand a swig for

the cook a match for you little brother o what a

zigzag rollercoaster this stygian journey flambéed you'll

be calmed with a rain of flour then moistened again with

brine added poco a poco (some cover you now with a slice

of white bread—meant, they say, to keep the wine

from coagulating) ninety minutes on a low fire &

you're done your limbs come to rest on a white platter

your blood & chopped raw liver now blended with fresh cream

add some of the sauce another glass of armagnac
now the rest of the sieved sauce carefully stir it all together
& off the fire & the pieces added the zigzag legs the sexy
saddles that was then & there my grandfather long ago called back
by the rabid gods we now live where they don't tell hares
from rabbits but our appetites are not diminished we will
eat 2 rabbits for a hare this is zigzag america after all it has old
it has new things it has the bitter it has the rich
and here now read how brother rabbit is done in our house
"our rabbit left thes…" & Nicole did this which she names after the
date of its invention

Birney Imes, *Rabbit hunters, Lowndes County, Mississippi 1980*

Conejo 25 de abril

(serves 4!)

- CUT THE RABBIT into 5 pieces (at first cut 3 pieces lengthwise then split legs in the middle. If you deal with a rather large rabbit cut the *râble* (saddle) in two pieces so you will have 6 pieces) and set aside.

- Soak 1 TOASTED CHILE PASSILLA in ½ cup DARK MEXICAN BEER (DOS EQUIS).

- In a pan sauté 2 CHOPPED MEDIUM ONIONS until they are golden, then add 1 CUP CHOPPED SUNDRIED TOMATOES (not rehydrated) mix them well with your wooden spoon & keep stirring until onions pick up the color of the tomatoes. Now add 8 KALAMATA OLIVES pitted and very roughly chopped; mix it up & let the ingredients sauté for a few minutes. It is now time to add 1 CAN OF TUNA FISH (Solid in Water), stir up and remove from the fire.

- Retrieve the soaking CHILE PASSILLA, cut stem and drain, chop it into pieces and work in the mortar as a paste incorporating 4 (degermed, thus belch free!) CLOVES OF GARLIC. When your paste is smooth add ½ CUP OF THE SAUTÉED ONION MIXTURE poco a poco and make it into a paste. Thin this paste with another ½ CUP OF DOS EQUIS. (This whole thing could be done in a food processor & would probably take ¹⁄₁₀ of the time. The taste however seems to be affected by the mechanical procedure.)

- Now comes my favorite part: in a DUTCH OVEN SKILLET heat 3 TABLESPOONS OF DUCK FAT (everybody has duck fat available in his fridge, right!) or, as a good substitute, about 3 TABLESPOONS OF VIRGIN OLIVE OIL. When *bien chaud* throw in the rabbit and golden it on all sides, then flambé with a little tequila, smell, mix well, add the chile mixture. Mix well, add the onion mixture, mix well. Add ANOTHER CUP OF BEER OR TWO—you will be the judge of the consistency— and then cook at *feu très très doux* (petit simmer) for at least 2 hours, check it once in a while, smell it all the time, do not turn on the fan of your stove but let the fumes take over the house.

- Serve in the cooking pot, accompanied by a steaming dish of quinoa.

P.S. Excellent organic rabbits available at 1-800-D'ARTAGN(AN).

III

CHICKEN, PORK, MUTTON, LAMB AND BEEF

A Good Meal

ERNEST HEMINGWAY

WE ATE DINNER at Madame Lecomte's restaurant on the far side of the island. It was crowded with Americans and we had to stand up and wait for a place. Some one had put it in the American Women's Club list as a quaint restaurant on the Paris quais as yet untouched by Americans, so we had to wait forty-five minutes for a table. Bill had eaten at the restaurant in 1918, and right after the armistice, and Madame Lecomte made a great fuss over seeing him.

"Doesn't get us a table, though," Bill said. "Grand woman, though."

We had a good meal, a roast chicken, new green beans, mashed potatoes, a salad, and some apple-pie and cheese.

"You've got the world here all right," Bill said to Madame Lecomte. She raised her hand. "Oh, my God!"

"You'll be rich."

"I hope so."

After the coffee and a *fine* we got the bill, chalked up the same as ever on a slate, that was doubtless one of the "quaint" features, paid it, shook hands, and went out.

"You never come here any more, Monsieur Barnes," Madame Lecomte said. "Too many compatriots."

Man Ray, *Mr. Knife and Miss Fork* (1944)

Chicken Paprikás

CARL RAKOSI

SORRY TO BE so slow to answer your call for my favorite recipe. Here it is…finally…for one of the greatest dishes of all time, Chicken Paprikás:

2 medium-sized onions, peeled and minced;

2 tablespoons oil or margarine;

1 plump chicken, about 3 pounds, disjointed, washed and dried;

1 large, ripe tomato, peeled and cut into pieces;

1 teaspoon salt;

1 heaping tablespoon of paprika,

1 green pepper sliced;

2 tablespoons plain yogurt;

1 tablespoon flour; egg dumplings;

2 tablespoons heavy cream.

Will make 4 servings.

1. Use a 4 or five quart heavy casserole with a tight-fitting lid. Cook the onions in the oil or margarine, covered, over a low heat for about five minutes until almost pasty but not browned.

2. Add chicken and tomato and cook, covered, for ten minutes.

3. Stir in paprika. Add ½ cup of water and the salt. Cook, covered, over very low heat for thirty minutes. In the beginning the small amount of water will produce a steam-cooking action. Toward the end of the 30 minute period, take the lid off and let the liquid evaporate. Then let the chicken cook in its own juices, taking care that it does not burn (if the chicken is tough, add a few tablespoons of water).

4. Remove chicken pieces. Mix the yogurt, flour and 1 teaspoon of cold water and stir in with the sauce until it is very smooth and of an even color. Add green pepper, replace chicken parts, adjust salt to taste. Put lid back on casserole and over very low heat, cook until done.
5. Before serving, whip in the heavy cream.
6. Serve with egg dumplings.

Recipe for Egg Dumplings
    1 egg
    3 tablespoons oil or margarine
    1 ½ cups flour
    one-third cup water
    1 teaspoon & 1 tablespoon salt

1. Mix egg, 1 tablespoon oil or margarine, one-third cup water and 1 teaspoon salt. Mix in the flour lightly. Work the mixture just enough to give it an even texture (about 3 minutes). Let it rest for 10 minutes.
2. Bring to a boil 3 quarts of water with 1 tablespoon of salt. Dip a tablespoon into the boiling water, to prevent sticking, and use it to gouge out pieces of dumpling mixture and drop them into the boiling water.
3. When the dumplings have all surfaced to the top, turn the heat off and remove them with a slotted spoon. Then rinse them with cold water and drain.
4. Heat the remaining two tablespoons of oil or margarine in a frying pan and lightly toss the drained dumplings in it for a few minutes. Sprinkle with salt to taste.

A dish worthy of poets…of good poets, that is. The others, let them batten on chitlings.

Two Chicken Dishes from Italy

DJUNA BARNES

THE FOLLOWLNG RECIPES, the favorites of the royal house of Italy, illustrate the simpliclty, the lack of "traditional etiquette" and the disregard of court rule, that has endeared them to their people. Indeed the Italians recount, without fear of being accused of *lèse-majesté,* the anecdote, now a legend, of that memorable day when young Phillip of Hesse, enamoured of the Princess Mafalda, and desirous of making all haste in the formalities attendant upon securing her in marriage, sought out her mother, and looking in vain through every room of the Villa Savoia, descended into the kitchen, there discovering her whipping up cakes for the king.

The King and Queen carry their simplicity to the divine point of not knowing they are simple. They lunch at eleven thirty in the morning. It is a thing no King or Queen has ever thought of doing. They explain this deviation from custom by the irrefutable argument that "This is when the King has hunger." And once, the Queen was heard murmuring in assembly that "A pinch of salt is better than a pound, but a pound of butter is far superior to a pinch," apparently utterly and delightfully unaware that the maxim might not be considered of national import! Nor is Quirenale, the official Royal Palace ever used, saving when court functions absolutely necessitate it.

Spaghetti, macaroni and ravioli are much in evidence on the King's table, next in favour is chicken. But though certainly a delicacy for a king, it is also often prepared in humbler kitchens, for in Italy, chicken is one of the less expensive meats. In cooking, olive oil is generally used, but butter takes its place and is more pleasing to the American palate.

In preparing ravioli, spaghetti and macaroni it is well to remember the words, not only of Cavaliere Amadeo Pettini, chef to the king and sponsor for the following recipes, but also of one Alfredo of Rome, he who is famed for his art in this matter, for even Italians can, and do, make lamentable mistakes with their *pasta.* Their advice is brief and identical: "There is a moment when *pasta* (paste) is *a point* as the French say, when in other words, it is neither underdone nor over cooked; that nice instant between failure and success, for it is no more than an instant. Ravioli, spaghetti etc., should have body, slightly resistant to the tooth. This only the Italian knows. It is why our *pasta* is not fully appreciated by the French and the American. The cooking of these edibles is a war between paste and chef. When the victory goes to the former it is utterly devoid of character, when however the victory goes to the chef, it is a poem."

It is this seemingly uninteresting food that is the marrow and backbone of Italy, and when well prepared is deservedly so.

CHICKEN ALLA SIGNORINA

Remove the breastbone and the ribs of the chicken, leaving the remainder whole. Clean the giblets, mince them fine, adding a small piece of calf's liver. Fry these ingredients in good fresh butter, until slightly brown, pouring over them, during the frying, a glassful of meat broth; remove from the fire and mix in two large spoonfuls of lean ham (cut into small cubes), the soft part of a roll, soaked in milk, fifty grams of minced mushroom, a spoonful of grated cheese, salt, pepper, chopped parsley, and the yolks of three eggs.

Stuff the chicken with this, sew it up, and cook it on a spit or in the oven, painting it during the roasting, with a brush dipped in the yolk of an egg beaten up with a little melted butter, over this sprinkle bread crumbs. Remove from the oven when it has acquired a fine crisp crust. Serve whole with currant jam.

— Cavaliere Amadeo Pettini,
Chef to the King of Italy

POLLO ALLA DIAVOLA

This dish is so named, say the Italians, because it must be so hot that he who eats of it, (it is seasoned with cayenne pepper and English mustard) feeling his mouth ablaze, will consign both cook and chicken to limbo.

The following method is more humane and is usually followed by the peasants.

Take a young chicken, cut off neck and feet. Cut it down the middle laying it flat and kneeding it as much as possible, removing any little bones that protrude. Wash it well and dry, then put it on a gridiron or in the oven. When it commences to roast, turn and baste it with a brush dipped in melted butter or olive oil, and season with salt and pepper. When one side has begun to take colour, turn and cook the other side, continuing to turn and baste, until done. If you have no cayenne, good white or black pepper will serve. Garnish with lettuce leaves.

Meat, My Husband

LYDIA DAVIS

MY HUSBAND'S favorite food, in childhood, was corned beef.

I found this out yesterday. We had visitors in our living room who were talking about food. They were talking about swordfish and fresh tuna, which they had had in an expensive restaurant the night before. Then they started talking about childhood foods. They asked what our favorite childhood foods had been. I told them several stories about whipped cream before they specified that they had meant cooked foods. They mentioned macaroni and cheese as an example.

I could not think of cooked food that I had liked but only cooked food that had bothered me as a child—okra, and slices of roast beef with veins in them.

But my husband had an answer. He said that his favorite food had been corned beef. One of our visitors immediately proposed that corned beef with an egg on it was even more appealing.

My husband still likes red meat,
though he knows it is not good for him. He ate in diners quite often before he knew me. He ate in two different diners, but preferred one. There he liked the hot roast beef sandwich in particular. He still likes a good piece of steak, or hamburger mixed with barbecue sauce and cooked outdoors on the small grill we have set up on our deck.

But I am the one who cooks most of his meals now, partly because I want to and partly because he is earning a large proportion of our money so it is only fair.

I make him meals with no meat in them at all. Often there is no seafood in them either, because seafood is also not good for him, and often no fish, because he does not like fish unless it is cooked in such a way that he cannot tell it is there, and often no cheese, because of the high fat content of most cheeses. I make him a brown rice casserole, for example, or winter vegetables with parsley sauce, or turnip soup with turnip greens, or white bean and eggplant gratin, or polenta with spicy vegetables.

Once I marinated slabs of tofu in tamari sauce, champagne vinegar, red wine, toasted marjoram, and dried Chinese mushrooms immersed in water. I marinated them for 4 or 5 days and then served them to him, sliced thin, in a sandwich with horseradish and mayonnaise, slices of red onion, lettuce and tomato. First he said the tofu was still very bland, which is what he always says about tofu, then he said that on the other hand he would not have been able to taste the tofu anyway because there were so many other things in the sandwich. He said it was all right, and he knew tofu was good for him.

He does not like what I cook quite as much as what he used to eat in diners and certainly not as much as what he used to make for himself.

For himself, for example, he used to make a roulade of beef cooked in a marsala sauce. He would take thin slices of top round or sirloin, dust them with flour, coat one side with crushed dill seeds, roll them around cooked Italian sausage meat, and pierce them with a

Claes Oldenburg, *Viandes* (1964)

CHICKEN, PORK, MUTTON, LAMB AND BEEF

toothpick. Then he would sauté them in butter and simmer them in a brown Marsala sauce with mushrooms. He would also make roulades of veal stuffed with prosciutto and gruyere.

Another favorite was a meatloaf of veal, pork, and sirloin. It would contain garlic, rosemary, two eggs, and whole wheat breadcrumbs. He would lay smoked bacon underneath it and on top of it. It was very rich.

Now I make him a loaf of ground turkey. It also has mushrooms, fresh whole wheat breadcrumbs and garlic in it, but in other ways it is not the same. It is made with one egg, celery, leeks, sweet red peppers, salt and pepper, and a dash of nutmeg. He eats it and says nothing, gazing out over the water past the willow tree. He is calm and contemplative. Perhaps he is calmer these days because of the way I am feeding him. He knows I am doing this for his own good.

When he says nothing about the turkey loaf, I question him, and when I press him to answer, he says that it is all right, but he is not excited about it. He excuses himself by saying he is not excited about food in general. I disagree, because I have seen him excited about food, though almost never about what I

serve him, more often about memories of food he has made himself. But once he was excited by what I served him.

It was the night I made polenta and spicy vegetables for our dinner. The polenta, spreading in a thick ochre circle under the heap of reddish-brown vegetables, looked strange on the plate. When he had eaten some of it, though, my husband said it tasted better than it looked—something he has said before about other meals of mine. The suggested dessert for this was a ripe pear, chilled, with walnuts. Before we sat down to our meal, I told my husband what I was planning for dessert, though I was not going to bother to chill the pear.

The fact is that I am not a very good cook, and one reason is that I do not understand the importance of detail and exactness in cooking. My husband does. When I told him my plan for dessert, he immediately put the pear in the freezer to chill while we ate the main part of the meal.

When we came to eat them, the contrast between the cool, juicy sweetness of the pear and the warmer, oily fragrance of the nuts certainly excited my husband, enough for him to imagine

other desserts of fruit—kiwis in liqueur, slices of blood orange with pecans, peaches and blueberries in a sauce of mint, lemon juice and sugar. Certainly he was more excited about this dessert than he later was about the turkey loaf, though it was also true that we were getting along better on the day of the pear and walnuts than on the day of the turkey loaf...

A Dull Dinner

CARL VAN VECHTEN

THE DINNER, as always, was simple: a soup, roast beef and browned potatoes, peas, a salad of broccoli, a loaf of Italian bread, pats of sweet butter, and cheese and coffee. Bottles of whisky, red and white wine, and beer stood at intervals along the unclothed refectory table. The cynical Tuscan butler, who had once been in the service of Lady Paget, never interrupted the meals to serve these. You poured out what you wanted when you wanted it. The dinner was dull....

Daniel Spoerri, *Marcel Duchamp's Dinner* (1964)

CHICKEN, PORK, MUTTON, LAMB AND BEEF

Pork à l'Alentejane

HENRI DELUY

ALENTEJO: *Além do Tejo,* beyond the Tagus, toward the South. A region which runs the length of Portugal, from Spain to the Atlantic Ocean and which touches, to the South, Algarve, land blessed by tourists. Vast stretches, more often than not flat. The chief wealth of the Alentejo, they say, is solitude. Evora, the sort of capital, is a very beautiful city. Region of agrarian reform, of peasants with raised fists. Region of fish, shellfish, pigs, olives and oil, cheese made from sheep's milk, and grapes.

To honor *Pessoa* (who didn't only like "bagaçau," the Portuguese marc, but was quite fond of it, it's true) and for our own pleasure, I propose two simple, easy to prepare dishes.

An Alentejane Salad:

Without removing the seeds, grill two or three beautiful, fleshy but not wrinkled red peppers, or roast them in the oven. Once grilled, you peel off the skin, remove the seeds, and cut them into strips. Add them to ripe-picked tomatoes, which have been peeled and cut into quarters. A tiny bowl of firm rice. A sauce made with crushed garlic, a teaspoonful of mustard, olive oil, and wine vinegar. Parsley. Very little salt, no pepper.

An Alentejane meat dish:

A small kilo of pork loin for 4 people. You cut the meat into pieces. You rub it with garlic paste (3 or 4 cloves), then with (watch out) a flour made from sweet red peppers. Let it sit, covered with a cloth, for 24 hours. At meal time, in a saucepan, you cook the slices of meat that you have cut again if you like, in crackling lard. You have washed and cleaned a kilo of one type of clams or another (for clams are always expensive!). After cooking your meat for 15 minutes, you put the clams, in another dish, on sustained heat with a glass or two of dry white wine, a laurel leaf, an onion cut into rounds, a sprig of parsley. When your clams have opened, your meat will be cooked. You serve the golden-brown slices of pork loin on a hot plate, with the clams on top, all lightly basted with the juice from the cooked clams. You add fresh, chopped coriander leaves, lemon juice. The Portuguese eat it with fries. Not me. It's amazing, hearty, it's a great, high quality dish.

Translated by Guy Bennett

Mutton

GERTRUDE STEIN

A LETTER which can wither, a learning which can suffer and an outrage which is simultaneous is principal.

Student, students are merciful and recognized they chew something.

Hate rests that is solid and sparse and all in a shape and largely very largely. Interleaved and successive and a sample of smell all this makes a certainty a shade.

Light curls very light curls have no more curliness than soup. This is not a subject.

Change a single stream of denting and change it hurriedly, what does it express, it expresses nausea. Like a very strange likeness and pink, like that and not more like that than the same resemblance and not more like that than no middle space in cutting.

An eye glass, what is an eye glass, it is water. A splendid specimen, what is it when it is little and tender so that there are parts. A center can place and four are no more and two and two are not middle.

Melting and not minding, safety and powder, a particular recollection and a sincere solitude all this makes a shunning so thorough and so unrepeated and surely if there is anything left it is a bone. It is not solitary.

Any space is not quiet it is so likely to be shiny. Darkness very dark darkness is sectional. There is a way to see in onion and surely very surely rhubarb and a tomato, surely very surely there is that seeding. A little thing in is a little thing.

Mud and water were not present and not any more of either. Silk and stockings were not present and not any more of either. A receptacle and a symbol and no monster were present and no more. This made a piece show and was it a kindness, it can be asked was it a kindness to have it warmer, was it a kindness and does gliding mean more. Does it.

Does it dirty a ceiling. It does not. Is it dainty, it is if prices are sweet. Is it lamentable, it is not if there is no undertaker. Is it curious, it is not when there is youth. All this makes a line, it even makes makes no more. All this makes cherries. The reason that there is a suggestion in vanity is due to this that there is a burst of mixed music.

A temptation any temptation is an exclamation if there are misdeeds and little bones. It is not astonishing that bones mingle as they vary not at all and in any case why is a bone outstanding, it is so because the circumstance that does not make a cake and character is so easily churned and cherished.

Mouse and mountain and a quiver, a quaint statue and pain in an exterior and silence more silence louder shows salmon a mischief intender. A cake, a real salve made of mutton and liquor, a specially retained rinsing and an established cork and blazing, this which resignation influences and restrains, restrains more altogether. A sign is the specimen spoken.

A meal in mutton, mutton, why is lamb cheaper, it is cheaper because so little is more. Lecture, lecture and repeat instruction.

Lamb à Lan

LYN HEJINIAN

One minute in a skull and the next in a belly, as Beckett says

A bowl set atop a female torso, the bowl serving as its head, sometimes with realistic details
which suggest that the bowl serves as a portrait of a person serving
The room that's all foreground
The odor is not ochre but rather a very red brown
Mumbling is very distinctly about something

olive oil
1 ½ pounds lamb, cubed (from shoulder, preferably; any lean cut for stew will do)
6 carrots, coarsely chopped
4 leeks, washed carefully and cut into small rings
2 large tomatoes, peeled and finely chopped
7 cloves of garlic, finely chopped
2 bay leaves
1 tsp. oregano
1 tsp. thyme

Heat 2–3 tablespoons of oil in a dutch oven and brown the lamb over high heat, a few pieces at a time. Remove the lamb as it is browned, and then let the dutch oven cool slightly before returning the lamb with the other ingredients to the dutch oven.

Place vegetables, spices, and lamb in the dutch oven, along with a cup or cup and a half (depending on the juiciness of the tomatoes) of water; or you may use half water and half good red wine. Let simmer in 350 degree oven for 2 hours, or until tender. If you use meat from the leg, it will be very tender and require only about an hour for cooking, but meat from the shoulder has more flavor. Check occasionally and add more liquid if necessary.

With red wine, a fresh green salad, and rice, this serves four to six people. You might squeeze a lime over the rice.

Farce Double

HARRY MATHEWS

COUNTRY COOKING
FROM CENTRAL FRANCE:
ROAST BONED ROLLED
STUFFED SHOULDER OF LAMB
(Farce double)

for Maxine Groffsky

HERE IS an old French regional dish for you to try. Attempts by presumptuous chefs to refine it have failed to subdue its basically hearty nature. It demands some patience, but you will be abundantly rewarded for your pains.

Farce double—literally, double stuffing—is the specialty of La Tour Lambert, a mountain village in Auvergne, that rugged heart of the Massif Central. I have often visited La Tour Lambert: the first time was in late May, when *farce double* is traditionally served. I have observed the dish being made and discussed it with local cooks.

The latter were skeptical about reproducing *farce double* elsewhere—not out of pride, but because they were afraid the dish would make no sense to a foreigner. (It is your duty to prove them wrong—and nothing would make them happier if you did.) Furthermore, they said, certain ingredients would be hard to find. Judicious substitution is our answer to that. Without it, after all, we would have to forgo most foreign cooking not out of a can.

The shoulder of lamb itself requires attention. You must buy it from a butcher who can dress it properly. Tell him to include the middle neck, the shoulder chops in the brisket, and part of the foreshank. The stuffing will otherwise fall out of the roast.

In Auvergne, preparing the cut is no problem, since whole lambs are roasted: the dish is considered appropriate for exceptional, often communal feasts, of a kind that has become a rarity with us.

All bones must be removed. If you leave this to the butcher, have him save them for the deglazing sauce. The fell or filament must be kept intact, or the flesh may crumble.

Set the boned forequarter on the kitchen table. Do not slice off the purple inspection stamps but scour them with a brush dipped in a weak solution of lye. The meat will need all the protection it can get. Rinse and dry.

Marinate the lamb in a mixture of 2 qts of white wine, 2 qts of olive oil, the juice of 16 lemons, salt, pepper, 16 crushed garlic cloves, 10 coarsely chopped yellow onions, basil, rosemary, melilot, ginger, allspice, and a handful of juniper berries. The juniper adds a pungent, authentic note. In Auvergne, shepherds pick the berries in late summer when they drive their flocks from the mountain pastures. They deposit the berries in La Tour Lambert, where they are pickled through the winter in cider brandy. The preparation is worth making, but demands foresight.

If no bowl is capacious enough for the lamb and its marinade, use a washtub. Without a tub, you must improvise. Friends of mine in Paris resort to their bidet; Americans may have to fall back on the kitchen sink, which is what I did the first time I made *farce double*. In La Tour Lambert, most houses have stone marinating troughs. Less favored citizens use the municipal troughs in the entrance of a cave in the hillside, just off the main square.

The lamb will have marinated satisfactorily in 5 or 6 days.

Allow yourself 3 hours for the stuffings. The fish balls or quenelles that are their main ingredient can be prepared a day in advance and refrigerated until an hour before use.

The quenelles of La Tour Lambert have traditionally been made from *chaste,* a fish peculiar to the mountain lakes of Auvergne. The name, a dialect word meaning "fresh blood," may have been suggested by the color of its spreading gills, through which it ingests its food. (It is a mouthless fish.) It is lured to the surface with a skein of tiny beads that resemble the larvae on which it preys, then bludgeoned with an underwater boomerang. *Chaste* has coarse, yellow-white flesh, with a mild but inescapable taste. It has been vaguely and mistakenly identified as a perch; our American perch, however, can replace it, provided it has been caught no more than 36 hours

before cooking. Other substitutes are saltwater fish such as silver hake or green cod. If you use a dry-fleshed fish, remember to order beef-kidney fat at the butcher's to add to the fish paste. (Be sure to grind it separately.)

To a saucepan filled with 2½ cups of cold water, add salt, pepper, 2 pinches of grated nutmeg, and 6 tbsp of butter. Boil. Off heat, begin stirring in 2½ cups of flour and continue as you again bring the water to a boil. Take off heat. Beat in 5 eggs, one at a time, then 5 egg whites. Let the liquid cool.

Earlier, you will have ground 3¾ lbs of fish with a mortar and pestle—heads, tails, bones, and all—and forced them through a coarse sieve. Do *not* use a grinder, blender, or cuisinart. The sieve of La Tour Lambert is an elegant sock of meshed copper wire, with a fitted ashwood plunger. It is kept immaculately bright. Its apertures are shrewdly gauged to crumble the bones without pulverizing the flesh. Into the strained fish, mix small amounts of salt, white pepper, nutmeg, and chopped truffles—fresh ones, if possible. (See *truffle.*)

Stir fish and liquid into an even paste.

Two hours before, you will have refrigerated 1 cup of the heaviest cream

available. Here, of course, access to a cow is a blessing.

The breathtakingly viscid cream of La Tour Lambert is kept in specially excavated cellars. Those without one use the town chiller, in the middle depths—cool but not cold—of the cave mentioned earlier. Often I have watched the attendant women entering and emerging from that room, dusky figures in cowls, shawls, and long gray gowns, bearing earthenware jugs like offerings to a saint.

Beat the cool cream into the paste. Do it slowly: think of those erect, deliberate Auvergnat women as they stand in the faint gloom of the cave, beating with gestures of timeless calm. It should take at least 15 minutes to complete the task.

At some previous moment, you will have made the stuffing for the quenelles. (This is what makes the stuffing "double.") It consists of the milt of the fish and the sweetbreads of the lamb, both the neck and stomach varieties. (Don't forget to mention *them* to your butcher.) The milt is rapidly blanched. The sweetbreads are diced, salted, spiced with freshly ground hot pepper, and tossed for 6 minutes in clarified butter. Both are then chopped very fine (blender permitted) and kneaded into an unctuous mass with the help of 1 cup of lamb marrow and 3 tbsp of aged Madeira.

I said at the outset that I am in favor of appropriate substitutions in preparing *farce double:* but even though one eminent authority has suggested it, stuffing the quenelles with banana peanut butter is not appropriate.

The quenelles must now be shaped. Some writers who have discoursed at length on the traditional Auvergnat shape urge its adoption at all costs. I disagree. For the inhabitants of La Tour Lambert, who attach great significance to *farce double,* it may be right to feel strongly on this point. The same cannot be said for families in Maplewood or Orange County. You have enough to worry about as it is. If you are, however, an incurable stickler, you should know that in Auvergne molds are used. They are called *beurdes* (they are, coincidentally, shaped like birds), and they are available here. You can find them in any of the better head shops.

But forget about bird molds. Slap your fish paste onto a board and roll it flat. Spread on stuffing in parallel ½-inch bands 2 inches apart. Cut paste midway between bands, roll these strips into cylinders, and slice the cylinders into sections no larger than a small headache. Dip each piece in truffle crumbs. (See *truffle.*)

I refuse to become involved in the pros and cons of presteaming the quenelles. The only steam in La Tour Lambert is a rare fragrant wisp from the dampened fire of a roasting pit.

We now approach a crux in the preparation of *farce double:* enveloping the quenelles and binding them into the lamb. I must make a stern observation here; and you must listen to it. You must take it absolutely to heart.

If the traditional ways of enveloping the quenelles are arduous, they are in no way gratuitous. On them depends an essential component of *farce double,* namely the subtle interaction of lamb and fish. While the quenelles (and the poaching liquid that bathes them) must be largely insulated from the encompassing meat, they should not be wholly so. The quenelles must not be drenched in roasting juice or the lamb in fishy broth, but an exchange should occur, definite no matter how mild. Do not *under any circumstance* use a baggie or Saran Wrap to enfold the quenelles. Of course it's easier. So are TV dinners. For once, demand the utmost of yourself: the satisfaction will astound you, and *there is no other way.*

I mentioned this misuse of plastic to a native of La Tour Lambert. My interlocutor, as if appealing for divine aid, leaned back, lifted up his eyes, and stretched forth his arms. He was standing at the edge of a marinating trough; its edges were slick with marinade. One foot shot forward, he teetered for one moment on the brink, and then down he went. Dripping oil, encrusted with fragrant herbs, he emerged briskly and burst into tears.

There are two methods. I shall describe the first one briefly: it is the one used by official cooks for public banquets. Cawl (tripe skin) is scraped free of fat and rubbed with pumice stone to a thinness approaching nonexistence. This gossamer is sewn into an open pouch, which is filled with the quenelles and broth before being sewn shut. The sealing of the pouch is preposterously difficult. I have tried it six times; each time, ineluctable burstage has ensued. Even the nimble-fingered, thimble-thumbed seamstresses of La Tour Lambert find it hard. In their floodlit corner of the festal cave, they are surrounded by a sizable choir of wailing boys whose task is to aggravate their intention to a pitch of absolute, sustained concentration. If the miracle always occurs, it is never less than miraculous.

The second method is to seal the quenelles inside a clay shell. This demands no supernatural skills, merely attention.

Purveyors of reliable cooking clay now exist in all major cities. The best are Italian. In New York, the most dependable are to be found in east Queens. (For addresses, see *Appendix*).

Stretch and tack down two 18-inch cheesecloth squares. Sprinkle until soaking (mop up puddles, however). Distribute clay in pats and roll flat until entire surface is evenly covered. The layer of clay should be no more than $\frac{1}{16}$ inch thick. Scissor edges clean.

Drape each square on an overturned 2-qt bowl. Fold back flaps. Mold into hemispheres. Check fit, then dent edge of each hemisphere with forefinger so that when dents are facing each other, they form a $\frac{3}{4}$-inch hole.

Be sure to prepare the shell at least 48 hours in advance so that it hardens properly. (If you are a potter, you can bake it in the oven; if not, you risk cracking.) As the drying clay flattens against the cheesecloth, tiny holes will appear. Do *not* plug them. Little will pass through them: just enough to allow the necessary exchange of savors.

Make the poaching liquid—3 qts of it—like ordinary fish stock (q.v.). The wine used for this in Auvergne is of a local sparkling variety not on the market; but any good champagne is an acceptable substitute.

By "acceptable substitute," I mean one acceptable to me. Purists have cited the fish stock as a reason for not making *farce double* at all. In La Tour Lambert, they rightly assert, the way the stock is kept allows it to evolve without spoiling: in the amphora-like jars that are stored in the coldest depths of the great cave, a faint, perpetual fermentation gives the perennial brew an exquisite, violet-flavored sourness. This, they say, is inimitable. *I* say that 30 drops of decoction of elecampane blossoms will reproduce it so perfectly as to convince the most vigilant tongue.

Fifteen minutes before roasting time, put the quenelles in one of the clay hemispheres. Set the other against it, dent to dent. Seal the seam with clay, except for the hole, and thumb down well. Hold the sphere in one hand with the hole on top. With a funnel, pour in *hot* poaching liquid until it overflows, then empty 1 cup of liquid. This is to keep the shell from bursting from within when the broth reaches a boil.

Be sure to keep the shell in your hand: set in a bowl, one bash against its side will postpone your dinner for several days at least. In La Tour Lambert, where even more fragile gut is used, the risks are lessened by placing the diaphanous bags in wooden reticules. It is still incredible that no damage is ever done to them on the way to the stuffing tables. To avoid their cooling, they are carried at a run by teen-age boys, for whom this is a signal honor: every Sunday throughout the following year, they will be allowed to wear their unmistakable lily-white smocks.

Earlier in the day, you will have anointed the lamb, inside and out: inside, with fresh basil, coriander leaves, garlic, and ginger thickly crushed into walnut oil (this is a *must*); outside, with mustard powder mixed with—ideally—wild-boar fat. I know that wild boars do not roam our woods (sometimes, on my walks through Central

Park, I feel I may soon meet one): bacon fat will do—about a pint of it.

You will have left the lamb lying outside down. Now nestle the clay shell inside the boneless cavity. Work it patiently into the fleshly nooks, then urge the meat in little bulges around it, pressing the lamb next to the shell, not against it, with the gentlest possible nudges. When the shell is deeply ensconced, fold the outlying flaps over it, and shape the whole into a regular square cushion roast. Sew the edges of the meat together, making the seams hermetically tight.

If the original roasting conditions will surely exceed your grasp, a description of them may clarify your goals.

In Auvergne, the body of the lamb is lowered on wetted ropes into a roasting pit. It comes to rest on transverse bars set close to the floor of the pit. Hours before, ash boughs that have dried through three winters are heaped in the pit and set ablaze: by now they are embers. These are raked against the four sides and piled behind wrought-iron grids into glowing walls. The cast-iron floor stays hot from the fire. When the lamb is in place, a heated iron lid is set over the pit. The lid does more than re-fract heat from below. Pierced with a multitude of small holes, it allows for aspersions of water on coals that need damping and the sprinkling of oil on the lamb, which is thus basted throughout its roasting in a continuous fine spray. Previously, I might add, the lamb has been rapidly seared over an open fire. Four senior cooks manage this by standing on high stepladders and manipulating the poles and extensible thongs used to shift the animal, which they precisely revolve over the flames so that it receives an even grilling.

Thus the onslaught of heat to which the lamb is subjected is, while too restrained to burn it, intense enough to raise the innermost broth to the simmering point.

Carefully lower the lamb into a 25-inch casserole. (If you have no such casserole, buy one. If it will not fit in your oven, consider this merely one more symptom of the shoddiness of our age, which the popularity of dishes like *farce double* may someday remedy.) Cover. You will have turned on the oven at maximum heat for 45 minutes at least. Close the oven door and lower the thermostat to 445°. For the next 5 hours, there is nothing to do except check the oven thermometer occasionally and baste the roast with juices from the casserole every 10 minutes. If you feel like catnapping, have no compunctions about it.

Do *not* have anything to drink—considering what lies in store for you, it is a foolish risk. The genial cooks of La Tour Lambert may fall to drinking, dancing, and singing at this point, but remember that they have years of experience behind them; and you, unlike them, must act alone.

One song always sung during the roasting break provides valuable insight into the character of the Auvergnat community. It tells the story of a blacksmith's son who sets out to find his long-lost mother. She is dead, but he cannot remember her death, nor can he accept it. His widowed father has taken as second wife a pretty woman younger than himself. She is hardly motherly toward her stepson: one day, after he has grown to early manhood, she seduces him—in the words of the song, "she does for him what mother never did for her son." This line recurs throughout as a refrain.

It is after the shock of this event that the son leaves in quest of his mother. His father repeatedly tries to dissuade him, insisting that she is dead, or that, if she is alive, it is only in a place "as near as the valley beyond the hill and far away as the stars." In the end, however, he gives his son a sword and a purse full of money and lets him go. The stepmother, also hoping to keep the son from leaving, makes another but this time futile attempt to "do for him what mother never did for her son."

At the end of three days, the son comes to a city. At evening he meets a beautiful woman with long red hair. She offers him hospitality, which he accepts, and she attends lovingly to his every want. Pleasure and hope fill his breast. He begins wondering. He asks himself if this woman might not be his lost mother. But when night falls, the red-haired woman takes him into her bed and "does for him what mother never did for her son." The son knows she cannot be the one he seeks. Pretending to sleep, he waits for an opportunity to leave her; but, at midnight, he sees her draw a length of strong, sharp cord from beneath her pillow and stretch it towards him. The son leaps up, seizes his sword, and confronts the woman. Under its threat, she confesses that she was planning to murder him for the sake of his purse, as she has done with countless travelers: their corpses lie rotting in her cellar. The son slays the woman with his sword, wakes up a nearby priest to assure a Christian burial for her and her victims, and goes his way.

Three days later, he arrives at another city. As day wanes, a strange woman again offers him hospitality, and again he accepts. She is even more beautiful than the first; and her hair is also long, but golden. She lavishes her attentions on the young man, and in such profusion that hope once again spurs him to wonder whether she might not be his lost mother. But with the coming of darkness, the woman with the golden hair takes him into her bed and "does for him what mother never did for her son." His hopes have again been disappointed. Full of unease, he feigns sleep. Halfway through the night he hears footsteps mounting the stairs. He scarcely has time to leap out of bed and grasp his sword before two burly villains come rushing into the room. They attack him, and he cuts them down.

Then, turning on the woman, he forces her at swordpoint to confess that she had hoped to make him her prisoner and sell him into slavery. Saracen pirates would have paid a high price for one of such strength and beauty. The son slays her, wakes up a priest to see that she and her henchmen receive Christian burial, and goes his way.

Another three days' journey brings him to a third city. There, at end of day, the son meets still another fair woman, the most beautiful of all, with flowing, raven-black hair. Alone of the three, she seems to recognize him; and when she takes him under her roof and bestows on him more comfort and affection than he had ever dreamed possible, he knows that this time his hope cannot be mistaken. But when night comes, she takes him into her bed, and she, like the others, "does for him what mother never did for her son." She has drugged his food. He cannot help falling asleep; only, at midnight, the touch of cold iron against his throat rouses him from his stupor. Taking up his sword, he points it in fury at the breast of the woman who has so beguiled him. She begs him to leave her in peace, but she finally acknowledges that she meant to cut his throat and suck his blood. She is an old, old witch who has lost all her powers but one, that of preserving her youth. This she does by drinking the blood of young men. The son runs her through with his sword. With a weak cry, she falls to the floor a wrinkled crone. The son knows that a witch cannot be buried in consecrated ground, and he goes his way.

But the young man travels no further. He is bitterly convinced of the folly of his quest; he has lost all hope of ever finding his mother; wearily he turns homeward.

On his way he passes through the cities where he had first faced danger. He is greeted as a hero. Thanks to the two priests, all know that it was he who destroyed the evil incarnate in their midst. But he takes no pride in having killed two women who "did for him what mother never did for her son."

On the ninth day of his return, he sees, from the mountain pass he has reached, the hill beyond which his native village lies. In the valley between, a shepherdess is watching her flock. At his approach she greets him tenderly, for she knows the blacksmith's son and has loved him for many years. He stops with her to rest. She has become, he notices, a beautiful young woman—not as beautiful, perhaps, as the evil three: but her eyes are wide and deep, and her long hair is brown.

The afternoon goes by. Still the son

does not leave. At evening, he partakes of the shepherdess's frugal supper. At nighttime, when she lies down, he lies down beside her; and she, her heart brimming with gladness, "does for him what mother never did for her son." The shepherdess falls asleep. The son cannot sleep; and he is appalled, in the middle of the night, to see the shepherdess suddenly rise up beside him. But she only touches his shoulder as if to waken him and points to the starry sky. She tells him to look up. There, she says, beyond the darkness, the souls of the dead have gathered into one blazing light. With a cry of pain, the son asks, "Then is my mother there?" The shepherdess answers that she is. His mother lives beyond the stars, and the stars themselves are chinks in the night through which the fateful light of the dead and the unborn is revealed to the world. "Oh, Mother, Mother," the young man weeps. The shepherdess then says to him, "Who is now mother to your sleep and waking? Who else can be the mother of your joy and pain? I shall henceforth be the mother of every memory; and from this night on, I alone am your mother—even if now, and tomorrow, and all the days of my life, I do for you what mother never did for her son." In his sudden ecstasy, the black-

smith's son understands. He has discovered his desire.

And so, next morning, he brings the shepherdess home. His father, when he sees them, weeps tears of relief and joy; and his stepmother, sick with remorse, welcomes them as saviors. Henceforth they all live in mutual contentment; and when, every evening, the approach of darkness kindles new yearning in the young man's heart and he turns to embrace his wife, she devotedly responds and never once fails, through the long passing years, to "do for him what mother never did for her son."

The connection of this song with *farce double* lies, I was told, in an analogy between the stars and the holes in the lid of the roasting pit.

When your timer sounds for the final round, you must be in fighting trim: not aggressive, but supremely alert. You now have to work at high speed and with utmost delicacy. The meat will have swelled in cooking: it is pressing against the clay shell harder than ever, and one jolt can spell disaster. Do not coddle yourself by thinking that this pressure is buttressing the shell. In La Tour Lambert, the handling of the cooked lamb is entrusted to squads of highly trained young men: they are solemn as pallbearers and dexterous as shortstops, and their virtuosity is eloquent proof that this is no time for optimism.

Slide the casserole slowly out of the oven and gently set it down on a table covered with a thrice-folded blanket. You will now need help. Summon anyone— a friend, a neighbor, a husband, a lover, a sibling, even a guest—so that the two of you can slip four broad wooden spatulas under the roast, one on each side, and ease it onto a platter. The platter should be resting on a short surface such as a cushion or a mattress (a small hammock would be perfect). Wait for the meat to cool before moving it onto anything harder. Your assistant may withdraw.

Meanwhile attend to the gravy. No later than the previous evening, you will have made 2 qts of stock with the bones from the lamb shoulder, together with the customary onions, carrots, celery, herb bouquet, cloves, scallions, parsnips, and garlic (see *stock*), to which you must not hesitate to add any old fowl, capon, partridge, or squab carcasses that are gathering rime in your deep freeze, or a young rabbit or two. Pour out the fat in the casserole and set it on the stove over high heat. Splash in enough of the same good champagne to scrape the casserole clean, and boil. When the wine has largely evaporated, take off heat, and add 2 cups of rendered pork fat. Set the casserole over very low heat and make a quick roux or brown sauce with 3 cups of flour. Then slowly pour in 2 cups of the blood of the lamb, stirring it in a spoonful at a time. Finally, add the stock. Raise the heat to medium high and let the liquid simmer down to the equivalent of 13 cupfuls.

While the gravy reduces, carefully set the platter with the roast on a table, resting one side on an object the size of this cookbook, so that it sits at a tilt. Place a broad shallow bowl against the lower side. If the clay shell now breaks, the poaching broth will flow rapidly into the bowl. Prop the lamb with a spatula or two to keep it from sliding off the platter.

Slit the seams in the meat, spread its folds, and expose the clay shell. Put on kitchen gloves—the clay will be scalding—and coax the shell from its depths. Set it in a saucepan, give it a smart crack with a mallet, and remove the grosser shards. Ladle out the quenelles and keep them warm in the oven in a covered, buttered dish with a few spoonfuls of the broth. Strain the rest of the liquid, reduce it quickly to a quarter of its volume, and then use what is left of the champagne to make a white wine sauce as explained on p. 888. Nap the quenelles with sauce, and serve.

If you have worked fast and well, by the time your guests finish the quenelles, the lamb will have set long enough for its juices to have withdrawn into the tissues without its getting cold. Pour the gravy into individual heated bowls. Place a bowl in front of each guest, and set the platter with the lamb, which you will have turned outside up, at the center of the table. The meat is eaten without knives and forks. Break off a morsel with the fingers of the right hand, dip it in gravy, and pop it into your mouth. In Auvergne, this is managed with nary a dribble; but lobster bibs are a comfort.

(Do not be upset if you yourself have lost all desire to eat. This is a normal, salutary condition. Your satisfaction will have been in the doing, not in the thing done. But observe the reaction of your guests, have a glass of wine [see below], and you may feel the urge to try one bite, and perhaps a second...)

It is a solemn moment when, at the great communal spring banquet, the Mayor of La Tour Lambert goes from table to table and with shining fingers gravely breaks the skin of each lamb. After this ceremony, however, the prevailing gaiety reasserts itself. After all, the feast of *farce double* is not only a time-hallowed occasion but a very pleasant one. It is a moment for friendships to be renewed, for enemies to forgive one another, for lovers to embrace. At its origin, curiously enough, the feast was associated with second marriages (some writers think this gave the dish its name). Such marriages have never been historically explained; possibly they never took place. What is certain is that the feast has always coincided with the arrival, from the lowlands, of shepherds driving their flocks to the high pastures where they will summer. Their coming heralds true spring and its first warmth; and it restores warmth, too, between the settled mountain craftsmen of La Tour Lambert and the semi-nomadic shepherds from the south. The two communities are separate only in their ways of life. They have long been allied by esteem, common interest, and, most important, by blood. Marriages between them have been recorded since the founding of the village in the year one thousand; and if many a shepherd's daughter has settled in La Tour Lambert as the wife of a wheelwright or turner, many an Auvergnat son, come autumn,

has left his father's mill or forge to follow the migrant flocks toward Les Saintes-Maries-de-la-Mer. Perhaps the legend of second marriages reflects a practice whereby a widow or widower took a spouse among the folk of which he was not a member. The eating of *farce double* would then be exquisitely appropriate; for there is no doubt at all that the composition of the dish—lamb from plains by the sea, fish from lakes among the grazing lands—deliberately embodies the merging of these distinct peoples in one community. I should add that at the time the feast originated, still another group participated harmoniously in its celebration: pilgrims from Burgundy on their way to Santiago de Compostela. Just as the people of La Tour Lambert provided fish for the great banquet and the shepherds contributed their lambs, the pilgrims supplied kegs of new white wine that they brought with them from Chassagne, the Burgundian village now called Chassagne-Montrachet. Their wine became the invariable accompaniment for both parts of *farce double;* and you could hardly do better than to adopt the custom. Here, at least, tradition can be observed with perfect fidelity.

It is saddening to report that, like the rest of the world, La Tour Lambert has undergone considerable change. Shepherds no longer walk their flocks from the south but ship them by truck. The lakes have been fished out, and a substitute for *chaste* is imported frozen from Yugoslavia. The grandson of the last wheelwright works in the tourist bureau, greeting latter-day pilgrims who bring no wine. He is one of the very few of his generation to have remained in the village. (The cement quarry, which was opened with great fanfare ten years ago as a way of providing jobs, employs mainly foreign labor. Its most visible effect has been to shroud the landscape in white dust.) I have heard, however, that the blacksmith still earns a good living making wrought-iron lamps. Fortunately, the future of *farce double* is assured, at least for the time being. The festal cave has been put on a commercial footing, and it now produces the dish for restaurants in the area all year round (in the off season, on weekends only). It is open to the public. I recommend a visit if you pass nearby.

Eat the quenelles ungarnished. Mashed sorrel goes nicely with the lamb. Serves thirteen.

Beefsteak with a Sweet-Sour Gravy

VÁCLAV HAVEL

We shortly and intensely roast a steak of beef on a frying pan with oil—in the usual way.

In a little pot we mix caramel, cranberry juice, soya sauce and red wine, add some salt and green pepper, water down and boil. Then we put into the pot a piece of butter and put the pot out of the stove. The butter will melt in the prepared mixture and produce the gravy that we pour on the meat.

We serve fried potatoes or chips as a garnish.

George B. Luks, *The Butcher Boy*

Staartstuk à la Frieda

HARRY MULISCH

Harry Mulisch mentioned a recipe of an old lady he used to be very fond of, Frieda Falk, his nanny.* In the Mulisch family this dish, which Sjoertje Mulisch prepares quite often, knowing it is her husband's favorite, is known as "Staartstuk à la Frieda." The "family secret" has just been handed over to me, and I shall try to give you a translation that will have to be adapted to American ingredients and measures. Here it comes.

—MARIJKE JALINK

---

* In her memory Harry Mulisch called his youngest daughter Frieda.

1 kg of rump
100 gr of bacon
1 liter of buttermilk
8 juniperberries
some laurel and peppergrains
a glass of wine vinegar
1 big onion
a piece of garlic

Cover the bottom of a dish, preferably a deep saucer, with sliced onion, the garlic, the laurel and the pepper grains and juniperberries which have to be crushed first. Put the piece of meat on these herbs and spices and pour the vinegar on it. Add the buttermilk in such a way that the rump is completely covered with the liquid. Put the dish in the fridge for a day and a half. Turn the rump of beef over and put it back in the refrigerator for another day and half. Dry the meat with a clean piece of cloth and pour the marinade in a large recipient. Put the bacon in the saucer, fry it out and take it out of the saucer in a cup. Add 50 gr of butter and fry the meat until it gets a nice brown color. Put the bacon back in the saucer, add the marinade and let it all simmer for about two hours. Strain the marinade, and thicken it with some maizena (maize flour?). Put the meat on a dish and add a cup of fresh cream to the sauce.

Cooking by Number

CHARLES BERNSTEIN

POETS don't have much time for eating—maybe the occasional slice of bread or cheese and then it's back to slaving over a hot word processor. (The greatest advantage of word processors may be that they force writers to air condition.) Sometimes it can take a few days of uninterrupted labor to write a single line of verse (it took me over three weeks of 17-hour days to pen the opening to one of my best-known unpublished works: "Now it is time for pastrami"). Given the lack of compensation for poetry (no wonder so much poetry is about lack, or lacking), there's hardly the money to buy food. Most of my food budget goes for coffee; in fact I believe a writer's most important tool is a PC— a personal capuccino machine.

I don't want to give the wrong impression. I worked as a culinary professional during the summer of 1970. I was salad chef at the Fenway Cambridge Motor Hotel. Smitty—Chef Smith—

was a charismatic person, who talked in deep bass tones with the sort of majesty that you don't associate with American life. This man used to slap a 20-pound rib roast on a delicatessen-style cutting machine, slicing off dozens of pieces of beef per minute to serve to the hundreds of waiting diners at one or another "function" that we catered. I also worked on the function crew. Once, Smitty told me to pour the salad dressing on the dozens of filled salad bowls that I had set up. I looked in the refrigerator and saw two huge metal pitchers filled with a whitish liquid dressing. It was only when Smitty couldn't find the yorkshire pudding mix that I realized what I had done. But then, no one complained and there was scarcely a piece of lettuce left in the bow(e?)ls at clean-up.

Our supervisor at Fenway Cambridge was Mr. Lopes, the Food and Beverage Manager. Mr. Lopes made it a point when he toured the kitchen never to cover his suit with an apron, just to make sure we knew he wasn't going to handle any food. Every day the first thing he would say to my friend Don Goldberg and me was "Gentleman, gentleman, the morning hasn't even started yet and already there's more breakage than anything."

The first two dishes I learned to make as a kid were meat sauce for spaghetti and pot roast. The pot roast recipe was from Peg Bracken's *I Hate to Cook Book* and consisted of pouring a bag of dry onion soup mix over the roast, covering with tin foil, and sticking in the oven. Like so many recipes: simple and none too good. But then it's hard to go wrong in cooking if you have good ingredients to start with—hard but not impossible. It's like that story Godfrey Cambridge used to tell about his wife showing up at some big affair completely naked except for a string of pearls. "But I read in the paper—you can never go wrong with basic black and pearls."

For advice about the stock market, I consult my astrologer; for advice about meat, I ask the butcher. I think a key to successful cooking is to establish a personal relationship with your butcher. These people know things that the rest of us are simply not privy to. My butcher— Emil at Endicott Meats on Broadway and 82nd street—sells me a whole brisket that he cuts into two first cuts and one beef stew. Now I like the second cut brisket but I get complaints at home about it—and if you push that sort of thing all you end up with is ulcers. This way the second cut can be stewed so long that you'd never know the animal had any fat on it.

Two of three packets I put in the freezer for later. Then I am faced with a dilemma. I've got to cook—messy business that it is. I recommend using an apron whenever you step into the kitchen—and I mean a full length one, which I think of as being something like those long-rider coats you see in the Westerns, only with brighter colors. Because the flour that you pour on the beef is bound to get all over you and the floor and the table—no way around it. Before I "flower" the meat, though, I usually put slivers of garlic under the fat and in the cracks. And I peel some onions, cut them in half, stick some cloves in. The flowered meat needs to be browned on all sides—and there's nothing wrong with doing that in a little olive oil. I use a big cast iron pan for the cooking. After browning, I fill up the pan with half wine and half water, up to the level of beef: too much liquid dries the thing out, too little and you've got nothing to pour on your rice for the next few days. (This last is an issue of almost Talmudic complexity but I don't have the space adequately to address it here). I toss the onions in, season with pepper, a tiny drop of salt, fresh parsley and dill, and oregano (yes that is odd but then there is very little else original about this recipe). After a while—you be the judge—I throw in some cut-up celery, carrots, maybe mushrooms. The whole thing needs to cook for at least two hours at a low simmer. It's even better the next day.

A Jean-Marie Cookbook

JEFF WEINSTEIN

I STOLE two cookbooks and read them when I knew I should be doing other things. I wanted to make a casserole of thinly-sliced potatoes, the non-waxy and non-baking kind, although the dish would be baked in cream. I found out from reading that what I wanted to do was no good unless I rubbed a clove of garlic around the inside of the pot, not that I'm adding the garlic itself, but that the cream seems to imbibe the flavor and hold it until you are ready. It was these fine points I wanted to know, the right and the wrong way to slice, the effective use of spices, why an earthenware dish "worked" (the way yeast "works") while a glass one didn't: the secrets of cooking. Some people argue that something should be done a certain way so it will taste a certain way, but how do they know that when they taste a dish they are all tasting the same thing? Experience makes a difference. For example, once I threw up when I ate a noodles and cheese casserole, so I won't eat one again, no matter how good. Experience even tells me how to feel about cooking something like a fried egg sandwich. I make them in bacon fat now, but for a long time I thought only big households with dirty tin cans filled with drippings, or a great constant cook like my friend Kit, could save baking fat and properly cook with it. For years I would throw the good clear fat down the drain, and I still don't know how or why I changed. It's like baking; I can't bake now, although I read baking recipes and work them through in my head, but only if I see that they apply to someone else, to someone *who can bake*. The most difficult transition I know is to move from one sort of state like that to another, from a person who doesn't bake to one who does. I would like to find out how it is done.

It seems that Jean-Marie took on the cloak of "gay" life in San Diego. He was a graduate student of art, interested in frescoes and teaching French on the side. Then, a year after he whispered he was going to remain celibate, mouthing the word as if he wasn't sure of the pronunciation, he started to skip classes. And one night he walked into the local gay bar, the one where people danced, called the Sea Cruise. At first he walked into the bar with women he knew from school and danced, commandeering them around the floor. Then he came with his old friend Mary, a head taller than he was, and they jerked around, absolutely matched. All this progressed over months; I would see Jean-Marie and Mary every time I was there, which probably means they were at the bar more often than I was. I can be sure they were always there together. I never ate dinner with them but I assume they would try to "taste" things the same way. Considering their need to think of themselves as alike, the idea of them kissing is interesting. They would want to think they were feeling the same thing, mutual tongues, mutual saliva. Their pleasure would not be mutual, and they would have to avoid thinking about that. Can you like kissing yourself? Can you like kissing someone you falsely imagine to be like yourself? It seems like deception to me, and I wonder why they do it.

*

Good cooking knives are indispensable to good cooking, which I learned by reading. I am told that carbon steel is better than stainless steel, that it wears away and gets more flexible with use, but such knives have to be dried after they are washed, their tips protected by corks, and you are supposed to yell at anyone who uses your knives for opening jars or other obviously damaging things. I don't mean to be facetious here, but apparently knives are important. I stole a set of Sabatier (lion?) knives that I thought were the best, stainless steel, but later I found out about the carbon versus stainless and got a sinking feeling in my stomach, though I also knew I would cherish them less and use them more.

Then Jean-Marie discovered men, or males rather, and started dancing with them, kissing them, and going out with them. The first was a sixteen year old boy whose personality was all Jean-Marie's idea, and every time they met his time was spent looking for it, the way

Puritans scanned nature to find signs of God. He and Jean-Marie probably did not sleep together, or if they did share a bed sometimes they probably didn't have sex. When this ended, by the boy leaving for San Francisco, Jean-Marie used disappointment as the excuse to pick up guys at the Sea Cruise, first the ones who liked to be mooned at, the quiet regulars, then the drugged-out ones, and then the ones made of stainless steel. He made the transition from gown to town by moving away from school to a dark house in the city, full of wood and plants and no light to read by. He slowly withdrew from the University and backed into San Diego, dropping old associations and living with a different opinion of himself. He sold his car so he could ride the municipal buses, and considered getting food stamps and general relief.

*

Here is a recipe I invented, a variation on scrambled eggs:

    2 eggs at room temperature
    cream, or half-and-half, sour cream,
        yogurt, though cream is best
    freshly ground black pepper
    a little salt
    butter (not margarine) unsalted but-
        ter is best

You take the eggs, beat them well but not frothy, then add a good lump (I call it a dollop) of cream or whatever, and *stir* it in. Grind in some pepper, add a little salt. Heat a good frying pan very slowly (this is important) and melt in it a dollop of butter. When the butter starts to "talk" add the egg mixture. Cook it slowly until it starts to curdle; this takes time, as it should, in the gentle heat. In the meanwhile get your toast ready and some tea. You can't rush this. Move the eggs around with a wooden spoon or fork; metal is not good. When they look done, creamy and solid, turn them into a warm plate. You may want to throw on some fresh chopped herbs, watercress, cilantro, parsley, but plain is wonderful. I don't know why these are a "variation" on scrambled eggs, but they do taste like no others. They even come out different every time, although some people can't tell the difference, and a few people I know won't even touch them.

*

When I met Jean-Marie on the bus he told me he got a poem published, and I suspected it was about love:

    His beating heart
    My moist lips, etc.
    It *was* about love, in rondelle form,

for he hadn't left school as much as he thought. The next night I had a friend over for dinner. I heard he was a gourmet so I was nervous to impress him, although I am not usually like that. Unfortunately I got home late and had to rush around to get everything ready, muttering to myself, but all at once I changed my mind about the matter and decided I was doing something which should be a pleasure, so I stopped worrying about it. Everything went well, basically because John wasn't much of a gourmet. We had: sherry, iced mushrooms with lemon juice and no salt, gratin dauphinois—a simple (hah!) casserole of thinly sliced washed dried new potatoes so thin that two pieces make the thickness of a penny, baked in a covered earthenware bowl rubbed with garlic, salted, peppered, and filled with cream. The cover is taken off towards the end of the baking so a brown crust forms. Eaten right away, and it was heaven. We were talking about Cretan art. It's important that the bowl be earthenware, that it be rubbed with garlic, and that the cream and potatoes come to within ¾ of an inch of the top of the uncovered casserole. We went up to the roof to grill the steaks and talked about the view and how odd it was to be in California. These steaks are called biftecks à la mode du pays de vaux, grilled and seasoned fillet steaks on a bed of chopped hardboiled eggs, fines herbes (I had only dried herbs but I reconstituted them if you know what I mean), lemon juice, and salt and pepper. I also added some chopped watercress. Then you heat it all. It was in this French glass dish I bought when I was so bored I could have killed myself. I stole the fillets. We drank wine and talked of sex. Then we had a salad of deveined spinach. He was really impressed; and I was surprised, both that he was so easily moved and that it all turned out so nicely. *I* was impressed too.

John brought a dessert, which was a home-baked apple pie, really a tart, and it was not as good as all that, but I was happy he brought it. It tasted much better the second day. We made out on the sofa then, but all of a sudden I got the urge to break away and go dancing, and John readily agreed. At the bar he fell "in love" with this beautiful Spaniard named Paco, who was drunk. They danced a lot together, badly, but John finally had to take me home. I wondered if he went back to meet Paco, but I thought not. John said he would see me when he got back from his trip to the East Coast. I had a dream that night in which I felt completely perverted and inhuman, and I think the meal had something to do with it.

*

Jean-Marie, after his year out in San Diego, wrote a long letter about promiscuity to *The San Diego Union,* which of course didn't get printed, although a month after he sent it in they lifted a small part of it and passed it off as opinion about a case where a lot of men got arrested in the bathroom of the San Diego May Company, "for indiscriminate reasons" the paper said.

Dear Sirs:

I am a gay male in San Diego and I want to talk about sex, or the problem of promiscuity so many of us face. Most of us, gay or not gay, are looking for someone to love, for a day, a year, or forever, and admittedly this is hard to do. But we have to try. However I don't understand why the only way many of the gay guys in San Diego try is by tricking. For those of you who don't know what tricking means, it's meeting someone, at a gay bar, in the park or on the street, going home and having sexual contact. Sometimes you don't even talk, because it would ruin everything. But when you do start conversations, they all go like this: what's your name (and you give your first name only), where are you from, what do you do, did you see…(a movie), etc., completely anonymous conversations, which is sad… Why do we do this? I don't really understand why, or why people hang around bathrooms, or even worse. It could be lust, but lust is just a screen for loneliness. Why doesn't the city of San Diego (or all cities) provide a place for people, gay and non-gay, to talk, dance, like a coffeehouse? This has worked elsewhere. But I do think that we as people should honestly question what they are doing. Sometimes I get so sick of what I am doing, going to bars every night, drinking when I don't want to drink, flirting when I don't want to flirt, staying out until two in the A.M. sweating and waiting for the right person, or at that point any person, that I don't know what to do. I could go back to the University but I know the University is worse. I wonder if I was roped into this. There are some people I meet at the gay bars that I really think should

be put away because of the way they act, and treat others. But other times I don't think that at all, and I just feel sorry for them. I wish I understood my appetites better, and I wish the city would do something about it.

*

I have never made a real dessert before, one that requires more than chopping up some fruits and adding whatever liqueurs I have around, so I thought I'd try something out of a cookbook, something called a chocolate bombe. I stuck to that one partly because I liked the name and partly because I like chocolate and also because I had some Mexican vanilla extract which would go well in it. "Chocolate Bombe" I realized later would make a good title for a screenplay, but it would have to be about food, and very few things are. Food is shown in some movies, like the gourmet concoctions in Hitchcock's *Frenzy* or the banquet in *The Scarlet Empress* or any number of bakery scenes with pastry on one side of the window and little faces, of boys usually, on the other. But nothing masterful or mature, and I don't think it's because food is silly or insignificant, but because it's hard to visualize people at a meal where food

stands for their relationships or essences in some way, like the beef dish in *To The Lighthouse*. How can I say I was "in the mood" to make something with cream, to watch something gel, to fill the beautiful mold sitting in the cupboard.

After I made the bombe, enough for ten people, there was so much left over that I left the key to my apartment outside the door and asked the couple in the next apartment to go into the freezer and help themselves, which they did, but other people helped themselves to my typewriter and television.

Chocolate Bombe (about ten servings)

Soak 1½ teaspoons of gelatin in one cup of cold water. Stir and bring to the boiling point 1 cup of milk, 1½ cups sugar, and two tablespoons of unsweetened cocoa. Dissolve the gelatin in the hot mixture. Cool. Add one teaspoon of vanilla extract. Chill until about to set. Whip 2 cups of cream until thickened but not stiff. Fold it lightly into the gelatin mixture. Still-freeze in a lightly-greased mold, and unmold ½ hour before serving.

It tasted rich, although there were too

many ice crystals in it. The best part was sampling the gelatin mixture before the cream was added, because it was so sweet and cold, just gelling, redolent of chocolate and Mexican vanilla. By the way, it doesn't come out tasting like pudding or jello; it's full of weight, like home-churned ice cream. It wasn't perfect, but because it came out at all I imagined it was better than it was.

Sometimes I eat because I'm lonely or disappointed. In fact, as I drive away from the bar at night, I tell myself (or the others in the car) it was "amusing" or "boring" or "kinda fun", but almost always at the same point in the turn to the main stretch home I feel a hollow feeling, which, when I recognize it, says I'm hungry, and I look forward to something to eat. It's almost absolutely predictable: the masking talk, the turn, and then the hunger, and often I overeat before I go to bed. The few times I've gone home with someone from the bar I've been really hungry the same way, so I assume these sexual episodes aren't really happy ones. Sometimes I've been nauseous, but that's a different feeling for different reasons. I've gone home with only one person who offered me a full breakfast in the morning or who

lived as if he cooked himself full meals. That was in New York City, with a very nice guy who just wanted to fuck me and get me to sniff amyl. He did get up early, and seemed to be making a lot of money, although the only thing I can remember about how he spent it was a really hideous gilt and glass table in his living room, and the fact that he bought towels at Bloomingdale's the afternoon before, spending more than a hundred dollars. The towels were hanging in the bathroom without even having been washed. We took a taxi home to his place, I remember now, I wasn't hungry and only slightly sick to my stomach. I ate underripe bananas with a guy I was "in love" with, but he was angry because I couldn't fuck him. And once, in Denver, the only thing I found in the refrigerator of this guy who picked me up, fucked me, and fell asleep at eight in the evening was one of those mealy chocolate flavored wafers you use to gain weight if you eat them with things or lose weight if you eat them alone. There was literally nothing else in there. I forgot about David. David made me a poached egg which tasted slightly of the vinegar in the water, on whole wheat toast, and fresh juice, and tea. I had many

more of those breakfasts, even though we didn't have sex, but I loved to sleep with David, and still would if we hadn't had that fight about the story I wrote once concerning him.

*

Jean-Marie became more and more bitter about his life, although he didn't realize to what extent he was excluding himself from his old friends, and especially from women. The world looks cruel when you concentrate only upon the males you know or want to know, and women become generalized and ignored, somehow peripheral. Jean-Marie got sick of this but he didn't know why, and one of his new friends could tell him. Certainly he was less stiff after a year in the Sea Cruise, and sloughed around the dance floor as if he had done it before, but...

But, he said, I'm special. I am a feminine man, and that's good, even better than being a woman. He would peer into mirrors, for mirrors were all over the walls of the rooms he haunted and play with disconnecting "Jean-Marie" from the little boy he grew up with. His head would twist and arch, one shoulder would rise, his nostrils flared as he imagined what could be possible. He never looked further down than his neck, and avoided parts of himself like his nose or the jut of his ears. Certainly he was bitter because he couldn't store this mirror-feeling, when his blood rushed and he could do anything. It wasn't vanity, this play in front of mirrors, nothing was being judged or compared, except perhaps the old with the new.

Oh ugh hmm. Do you really think so? Really I couldn't how could I? It wouldn't work...do you think so? Hmmm well. In far Peru there lived a llama he had no papa he had no mama he had no wife he had no chillun he had no use for penicillin...Jesus...yes of course I can come when do you want me...the bric please...fine I'll leave anytime of course but will they understand my English yes I know how important it is...God you're cute and you've gained weight hummph why do I get so much pleasure out of this...it's true isn't it.

*

I have made some bad errors in cooking, but these aren't nearly as important as errors in menu, or rather in the meal. I just heard of someone who swallowed a handful of aspirin, which made her sick. People are constantly eating to make themselves sick, to poison themselves, poison others, to forget, or to die. Someone once said stupidity takes corporeal form. I seem to have an aptitude for planning a happy meal, the combination of people, appetites, and what I call the "attitude" of the food: the amounts, the way a hot dish is followed by a cool one, the interplay or colors, the sequence of dishes and their values. I do this best when I am alone because people eating at my house sometimes make me nervous, and although I plan the food, I can never plan the run of old friendships at a dinner table. There's a whole history of ruining meals; in certain places, if you wanted to get even with a family you ground up the bones of their bird or some other possession into the food you served to them —it's a way of breaking up hospitality. One example of this was a stew which consisted of the guests' children. People no longer realize the potential power in the act of sharing food, but they do suffer the consequences whether or not they're aware of it. The menu of the most awful meal I ate:

mulligatawny soup and saltines
three bean salad

"oven-fried" chicken, I had the drumstick
mashed potatoes
green beans with butter
white bread and butter
ice cream and sugar wafers

There was something wrong with the soup but I didn't know what; it tasted bitter, not from any single ingredient but from the expression on the face of the person who stirred it. Really. It was bitter exactly the way a person is, in its "sweat". After the soup I said something nasty to a guest who was invited just to meet me, and everyone was embarrassed and tried to cover up. Mel belched out loud and George got annoyed but didn't say anything; he merely stabbed at his chicken and pushed it away. Judy spilled her milk on my pants, accidentally I'm sure, so I had to get up and change. When I got back George wasn't speaking to Nancy, and Mel was winking and nodding with no subtlety at all across the table. It could be that there were too many of us in the room, but we all had the same bad taste in our mouths.

I once had breakfast (brunch) in a gay bar, waiting an hour for a plate of bacon, two vulcanized eggs, and the pre-hashed potatoes that get scraped around a hot surface for a few minutes until their fetid water evaporates and they take on some color. Someone I didn't know was rubbing my knee and my only friend there kept drinking those morning drinks that make you anticipate evening, while the air smelled of the night before. How could I eat? I did eat, ravenously, but managed only by insisting to myself that except for my appetite I wasn't at all like the others around me. How long would that last? One more meal there could do the trick, so I swore I'd never eat at that bar again. I went home alone and looked at myself in the mirror to see if I had changed, for the grease from the potatoes was already beginning to appear on my forehead.

My God no. If you put a flower in a vacuum all its essence leaves. The fog might just be getting tired and collapsing into puddles…grease…damp… those little flakes of skin sticking in patches, nothing to show for all that reading, nothing to wear that fits, too big or too small and who can keep up with all that sewing even when I sew it unravels around my stitches. I'll throw it all out.

*

Two Mirror Snacks

1) bacon fat or a mixture of butter and oil, not too much

a few small potatoes, boiled in their skins

(leftovers are best)

one or two peeled and crushed cloves of garlic

the pulp, fresh or canned, of one tomato

plenty of basil

optional: cut pitted black olives, about 6

a few sliced mushrooms

a few celery leaves

Heat the fat or oil and butter in a small frying pan until very hot, put in the potatoes and mix them around, breaking them into chunks but not mashed. Add the garlic and some coarse salt if you have it, stirring constantly until they take on some color. Add the rest of the ingredients in any order you like (I add the olives last). Don't stir towards the end, so the bottom burns a little. Turn out onto a plate, add salt and freshly ground black pepper to your taste, and eat with white wine or beer. Be sure to scrape all the burnt particles and grease out with a spoon and eat them.

2) (you need a blender for this one)

an egg

a few big spoonfuls of plain yogurt

enough wheat germ to cover it, but not more than a tbsp.

a good ripe banana, broken into pieces

one cup of any mixture of: milk, half & half, fruit juice

½ tsp. of real vanilla extract (try Mexican vanilla)

some sweetener, honey, sugar, ice cream, just a bit

optional: a few spoons of protein powder

a spoon of soy lecithin

a tsp. of polyunsaturated flavorless oil

Add to the blender in the order mentioned, but don't fill to more than ⅔ capacity. Most protein powder tastes awful, so add only as much as you think you need. Non-instant dried milk is a good substitute. Blend at low speed for a few seconds, uncover, make sure the wheat germ isn't sticking in clumps to the yogurt, and scrape the now agglutinated protein powder off the sides of the blender and repulverize, all with a rubber spatula. Smell it, taste it, add more of what you think it needs. Cover and blend at medium speed for half a minute.

Have right away or refrigerate, but it will settle. Sometimes I add an envelope of chocolate flavored instant breakfast or some powdered chocolate because the chocolate and orange juice (if that's your juice) taste great together. Fruit jam is also good. Obviously this recipe can take a lot of things, but remember your purpose.

Note that each mirror snack is a different response to feeling bad.

*

In his response to the bar, or in his response to the person he was afraid of becoming, Jean-Marie resorted to interests connected neither to the school nor to the bar life he was now trying to avoid. He taught himself to knit, but when he found himself mooning over pictures of models in scarves and sweaters, he realized he didn't want to. Then he thought he'd learn to cook, revolted by the cold stupid meals he fixed for himself and by his unquestioning dependence on others for anything hot. One evening he had dinner with some of his University friends, baked ham and guacamole salad, for old times' sake. After dinner Jean-Marie asked them to try and describe the worst meal each of them could remember. He was stunned by his boldness—he never started things

but he was comfortable after the food and sat back to listen.

As they talked, Jean-Marie thought this was the most interesting conversation he'd heard since he left the University. He hated school, hated the lab scientists and art professors and the pretty jock behind the locker room cage who demeaned every woman as soon as she walked away. Yet even though the gay people at the Sea Cruise were gentle, they were more miserable with their lives than any group of people he knew. It was "they" now, but tomorrow it could be "we." What could he do? Could he straddle the two and possibly be happy? He was beginning to guess that happiness isn't the issue here, and survival is more crucial. "In what way" he thought "is survival related to being happy?"

*

The most difficult dishes in any cookbook are the "everyday" recipes, luncheon, bruncheon, egg, family dishes, cooking for survival when you have more important things to do or don't have much money. Let's assume you don't have a family to feed but haven't much time and want to be happy with what you are eating. Here is a list of staples for "everyday" meals:

milk

eggs, bought fresh a few at a time if possible

onions

oil or bacon drippings (bacon)

a little butter, unsalted

tomatoes, fresh and canned

garlic

cheap greens, vegetables in season

some cheese

bread, or flour to bake it

fresh boiling potatoes

chicken, all parts of it

lemons, possibly oranges

salt, black pepper

beer or wine

Staples are defined here not as what you need, but as what holds things together. I know this list assumes there is an "everyday." Some people, I know, have to cadge their next meal, for a place to prepare it, for a place to eat. These are people you should ask in for a meal, if possible.

I asked Jean-Marie to dinner. We agreed, although I don't remember why, to have a cooking contest. The rules were to prepare a menu. We would each cook our own menu and then each other's, which would take four nights. We de-

CHICKEN, PORK, MUTTON, LAMB AND BEEF

cided on a judge who needed the meals but who also understands more about food than anyone we knew without being disgusting.

Jean-Marie's menu, using the staple list, one good piece of flesh or fowl, some extra money, and one day's work:

consommé, iced, with chervil
carrotes marinées
boned leg of lamb, mustard coating
    (gigot à la moutard)
boiled new potatoes with parsley butter
sliced iced tomatoes with basil and
    olive oil
orange pieces flambé
café expresso
the meal is served with "a good French red wine"

My menu, with the same "limitations":

cream of potato and watercress soup
stuffed mushrooms
cucumbers and lemon juice
roast duck with tangerine stuffing,
    lemon curd glaze
parsley garnish

garlic mashed potatoes
spinach and cilantro salad, lemon
    juice dressing
strawberry lemon ices
the meal is served with cold Grey Riesling (California)

See appendix for comments on the selections. These are expensive meals, requiring not only food but many utensils and a lot of heat and cold (energy).

Jean-Marie and I met our judge, J., at my house the first evening, where I cooked my menu. J. said very little as we ate, although at one point he asked me for my recipe for stuffed mushrooms and their history:

Edythe's Stuffed Mushrooms
"My mother invented these one night when she ran out of clams to stuff. My father was rather demanding about the food their party guests (or rather his party guests) were served, and although my mother prided herself on her stuffed clams, it was still sort of slavework for her. This is not to say that my father didn't like to cook—he did—but he would not clean up after his filth, to use my mother's words. She liked these mushrooms, which were moist and

tasty, and I took her recipe and adjusted it to my tastes:

large open mushrooms, the bigger
    the better, 3 per person
at least one bunch of parsley
juice of one lemon
6 or so cloves of garlic, peeled
one or two cans of minced clams,
    drained
seasoned bread crumbs, Italian style
basil, fresh or dried
coarse salt
freshly ground black pepper
olive oil
plenty of freshly grated parmesan
    and/or romano cheese

The reason the quantities are vague is because I never measured them; the frying pan, a good heavy one, should determine the amount of everything. It almost always works out, and any leftover stuffing is delicious, although it should be refrigerated so you don't get food poisoning. The tricky part of this dish is making sure the mushrooms don't dry out, and all the soaking is for this purpose. Carefully twist the stems out of the mushrooms, so you are left with the intact cap and gills. Reserve the stems. With a spoon scrape the gills and all excess stuff out of the caps, so you are left with little bowls. As you finish this process, eating any mushrooms you may have broken, place the caps in a large bowl of cool water into which you've squirted the lemon juice. The mushrooms will soak in this; the acid prevents them from turning too brown. Mince the parsley flowerettes. Mince the garlic. Now, take each mushroom stem, chop off and discard the woody half, the part which stuck in the ground, and dice the remaining halves. Grate your cheese. Heat the frying pan slowly, then add at least ¼ inch of olive oil. This may seem like a lot, but it's necessary. When the oil gets fragrant, add the garlic. Before the garlic browns, add the clams and saute. Add the minced mushrooms, stirring constantly, the parsley, and keep cooking. Make sure nothing burns. Add salt, pepper, and enough breadcrumbs to soak up the excess clam and mushroom liquid. The basil should have been crushed and thrown in some time before; do add quite a bit. The stuffing should now be loose and moist but not liquid, and very hot. Remove from heat, and add most of your grated cheese, reserving some. Stir it all, and put it aside.

If you think the mushrooms have soaked long enough, take each one out, shake out the water, and with a spoon put the stuffing in. Do this with a light hand and keep the stuffing as particulate as possible. Stuff all the mushrooms. Now, if you must, you can leave them sit for a while (do not refrigerate), but it is best to put them immediately into a lightly greased broiling dish, having preheated your oven or broiler some time before, arrange touching in some kind of pattern, salt the tops, sprinkle with grated cheese and maybe a little olive oil, and run them under a hot broiler or in a very hot oven until both the stuffing is completely heated and the tops of the caps are not too tough and brown; it is an exact point. By that time the water in the mushrooms should have just steamed them, so they are perfectly cooked, neither raw nor brittle nor rubbery and slick. If you want to be fancy, place the mushrooms, before you broil them, on a bed of carefully washed and deveined leaves of spinach, and broil them together. Some of the mushroom juice will run out onto the perfectly cooked spinach, which can be used to sop it all up."

On the first evening Jean-Marie paled

a bit when he tasted my mushrooms, perhaps because he didn't know how easy they were to make. On the second night Jean-Marie cooked, and we both knew our food was good, so this time we talked nicely and forgot the pretense of competition.

"But I know Louis the 15th had a head shaped like a pear."

I should note that I did not tell our judge who cooked what. J. ate well, asking us to save portions of everything, so by the fourth night there should be two versions each of two different meals, three in miniature. Of course we were sickened at the prospect of so much rich food, but the concept of a cooking contest was still strange enough to be interesting. On the fourth night we talked about writing cookbooks and tasted a little bit of everything. Jean-Marie managed to make the mushrooms but could not even fake the ices, and my version of his marinated carrots was pale and sticky.

I say this in retrospect because at some point in our meal I couldn't tell what food was mine, or where it came from. Jean-Marie looked contemplative and sick. Our judge was so quiet we didn't see him most of the time. The courses were served by ghosts. Critical faculties must have faded, and we thought only of parody and death.

The grotesque prudishness and archness with which garlic is treated in this country has led to the superstition that rubbing the bowl with it before putting the salad in gives it sufficient flavor. It rather depends whether you are going to eat the bowl or the salad.

Jean-Marie left, J. left, I was left sitting alone not knowing when they had gone. There was a note:

I cannot tell the difference among your dishes because each bite was a universe. Why do you insist so much on difference and comparison? I was so happy to be eating, and it was all good food, that my joy overran any pose of judgment. When you cook something, and put it aside, how do you know who cooked it? Who were you that day? Who could have doctored the food, soured it, stolen it away and left a note of gibberish in its place? Certainly, you can write a cookbook, but could it possibly predict a meal? It's an odd mirror to stare into, with no certainty in it. There was

a point when I almost swallowed a bone, and some sherbet dribbled down my chin and stained the tablecloth. Did you notice? Would you have cooked that meal, or any meal, if I hadn't been there to eat it? Will your tablecloth wash out? (No matter, I blotted up the spill.) I do think you expect too much, but I would be pleased if you arranged your life so you could continue to cook. However I don't see that a cookbook could be anything but a reflection of imagined life, which is not a bad thing. I'd be happy to visit you again.

APPENDIX

Jean-Marie comments on his menu:

My menu is mainly French, relying on the good fresh vegetables of Southern California. The cold soup whets your appetite, the marinated carrots, which is a French country specialty, excites your now raging hunger and prepares your palate for the mustard flavor of the lamb. After all that cold stuff, the lamb and hot simple potatoes are a happy change. The red wine supports and is not pushed over by the strong flavors of the main dish. People should be talking at this point, as soon as the initial gobbling

has stopped. The iced tomatoes provide color, if the conversation doesn't, and the basil is yet another welcome flavor. After a pause (which I never think is long enough) the oranges cool your mouths, "degrease them" so to speak, and the espresso should be strong and black.

Comments on the other menu:

These are things I like. If the duck doesn't smoke up the whole house it can be quite a surprise, because people don't expect duck the way they expect chicken or lamb. The spinach and cilantro salad is also a surprise (especially if you don't wash the spinach enough) but seriously people see the blue-green leaves of the spinach and think it's lettuce but the light is funny, and then the cilantro, a lighter yellow-green, flashes like little bits of afterglow or whatever that visual phenomenon is called. And when they eat it, it's the same thing, because all the bland cuddy spinach juice is punctuated by the herb, utterly unexpected. Ices cool everyone after the duck. The menu works; I don't have to explain exactly why, do I? By the way, Jean-Marie shouldn't repeat the mustard of the carrots in his lamb.

Dessert

August Sander, *Pastry Chef, Cologne* (1928)

⊗

Apples, Figs, Raisins

GUNNAR GUNNARSSON

Paul Cadmus, *Apple Peeler* (1959)

THAT WAS what I would call myself: Hugleik the Reckless Sailor. I savored the name. Yes, that was the name under which I would certainly sail. My ship would have a dragon-head and a dragon-tail, and striped homespun sails as wings, and with this ship I would sail as no one had ever sailed before.

First of all, I would sail to that land, Brazil, and when I had spoken to Sophia's brother in all the eight languages that he understood, and eight others besides that he did not understand, I would fill the ship with apples, figs, and especially raisins, for my father liked them so much, and then I would take a trip on the blue sky; and when I arrived just above Grimsstadir, I would loose the whole cargo and shower it over the homestead (it would, of course, be best if it were in the middle of the hay harvest) and I would let red and yellow apples rain round my mother, raisins over my father, figs over Veiga, prunes over Beta, soft sugar over Madame Anna, biscuits over Nonni, barley-sugar over Maggi, currants, like sweet tears, over Maria Mens, coffee-beans over Disa and wrinkled oranges and books of sermons and other Words of God over Old Begga.

Fruits of Paradise

AKSEL SANDEMOSE

I HAD a secret place for apples, an ingenious little cache behind a pigeon's nest.

It might be that my children would say "No, thanks," to an apple. They had the strength to decline. I had not. For me fruit was like the symbolical apples which grew in the Garden of Eden: I was forever thirsting after it. I recall the thrill of excitement I never failed to experience upon gazing into an apple orchard, and I remember my painful hours in school as I watched Fröken Nibe gobbling up fruit as she walked to and fro in the classroom. I remember the crunching sound as her teeth bit into an apple, I can still see her before me ripping the skin from a plum. One of us would have to carry the skin and the pit from the room, and how that boy would lick at it as soon as he was outside the door! Thirty pair of eyes would follow Fröken Nibe. One day her cupboard was broken into. Fröken Nibe was appalled and the sin involved in that deed has survived to this day.

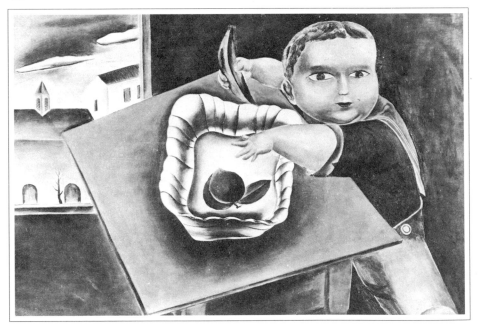

Yasuo Kuniyoshi, *Boy Stealing Fruit*

Wine Jellies

THOMAS PYNCHON

MRS. QUOAD'S is up three dark flights, with the dome of faraway St. Paul's out its kitchen window visible in the smoke of certain afternoons, and the lady herself tiny in a rose plush chair in the sitting-room by the wireless, listening to Primo Scala's Accordion Band. She looks healthy enough. On the table, though, is her crumpled chiffon handkerchief: feathered blots of blood in and out the convolutions like a floral pattern.

"You were here when I had that horrid quotidian ague," she recalls Slothrop, "the day we brewed the wormwood tea," sure enough, the very taste now, rising through his shoe-soles, taking him along. They're reassembling…it must be outside his memory…cool clean interior, girl and woman, independent of his shorthand of stars…so many fading-faced girls, windy canalsides, bed-sitters, bus-stop good-bys, how can he be expected to remember? but this room has gone on clarifying: part of whoever he was inside it has kindly remained, stored quiescent these months outside of his head, distributed through the grainy shadows, the grease-hazy jars of herbs, candies, spices, all the Compton Mackenzie novels on the shelf, glassy ambrotypes of her late husband Austin night-dusted inside gilded frames up on the mantel where last time Michaelmas daisies greeted and razzled from a little Sèvres vase she and Austin found together one Saturday long ago in a Wardour Street shop.…

"He was my good health," she often says. "Since he passed away I've had to become all but an outright witch, in pure self-defense." From the kitchen comes the smell of limes freshly cut and squeezed. Darlene's in and out of the room, looking for different botanicals, asking where the cheesecloth's got to, "Tyrone help me just reach down that— no next to it, the tall jar, thank you love"—back into the kitchen in a creak of starch, a flash of pink. "I'm the only one with a memory around here," Mrs. Quoad sighs. "We help each other, you see." She brings out from behind its cretonne camouflage a great bowl of candies. "*Now,*" beaming at Slothrop. "Here: wine jellies. They're prewar."

"Now I remember you—the one with the graft at the Ministry of Sup-ply!" but he knows, from last time, that no gallantry can help him now. After that visit he wrote home to Nalline: "The English are kind of weird when it comes to the way things taste, Mom. They aren't like us. It might be the climate. They go for things we would never dream of. Sometimes it is enough to turn your stomach, boy. The other day I had had one of these things they call 'wine jellies.' That's their idea of *candy,* Mom! Figure out a way to feed some to that Hitler 'n' I betcha the war'd be over *tomorrow!*" Now once again he finds himself checking out these ruddy gelatin objects, nodding, he hopes amiably, at Mrs. Quoad. They have the names of different wines written on them in bas-relief.

"Just a touch of menthol too," Mrs. Quoad popping one into her mouth. "Delicious."

Slothrop finally chooses one that says Lafitte Rothschild and stuffs it on into his kisser. "Oh yeah. Yeah. Mmm. It's great."

"If you *really* want something peculiar try the Bernkastler Doktor. Oh! Aren't you the one who brought me those lovely American slimy elm things, maple-tasting with a touch of sassafras"

"Slippery elm. Jeepers I'm sorry, I ran out yesterday."

Darlene comes in with a steaming pot and three cups on a tray. "What's that?" Slothrop a little quickly, here.

"You don't really want to know, Tyrone."

Edward Ruscha, *Jelly* (1964)

"Quite right," after the first sip, wishing she'd used more lime juice or something to kill the basic taste, which is ghastly-bitter. These people are really insane. No sugar, natch. He reaches in the candy bowl, comes up with a black, ribbed licorice drop. It looks safe. But just as he's biting in, Darlene gives him,

and it, a peculiar look, great timing this girl, sez, "Oh, I thought we got rid of all *those*——" a blithe, Gilbert & Sullivan ingenue's *thewse*—"*years* ago," at which point Slothrop is encountering this dribbling liquid center, which tastes like mayonnaise and orange peels.

"You've taken the last of my Marmalade Surprises!" cries Mrs. Quoad, having now with conjurer's speed produced an egg-shaped confection of pastel green, studded all over with lavender nonpareils. "Just for that I shan't let you have any of these marvelous rhubarb creams." Into her mouth it goes, the whole thing.

"Serves me right," Slothrop, wondering just what he means by this, sipping herb tea to remove the taste of the mayonnaise candy—oops but that's a mistake, right, here's his mouth filling once again with horrible alkaloid desolation, all the way back to the soft palate where it digs in. Darlene, pure Nightingale compassion, is handing him a hard red candy, molded like a stylized raspberry …mm, which oddly enough even tastes like a raspberry, though it can't begin to take away that bitterness. Impatiently, he bites into it, and in the act knows, fucking idiot, he's been had once more, there comes pouring out onto his tongue

the most godawful crystalline concentration of Jeez it must be pure nitric acid, "Oh mercy that's really *sour*," hardly able to get the words out he's so puckered up, exactly the sort of thing Hop Harrigan used to pull to get Tank Tinker to quit playing his ocarina, a shabby trick then and twice as reprehensible coming from an old lady who's supposed to be one of our Allies, shit he can't even *see* it's up his nose and whatever it is won't dissolve, just goes on torturing his shriveling tongue and crunches like ground glass among his molars. Mrs. Quoad is meantime busy savoring, bite by dainty bite, a cherry-quinine *petit four*. She beams at the young people across the candy bowl. Slothrop, forgetting, reaches again for his tea. There is no graceful way out of this now. Darlene has brought a couple-three more candy jars down off of the shelf, and now he goes plunging, like a journey to the center of some small, hostile planet, into an enormous bonbon *chomp* through the mantle of chocolate to a strongly eucalyptus-flavored fondant, finally into a core of some very tough grape gum arabic. He fingernails a piece of this out from between his teeth and stares at it for a while. It is purple in color.

Bonbons

MALCOLM DE CHAZAL

ONLY LIQUIDS can be tasted by the underside of the tongue. As the bonbon begins to liquefy, the back of the tongue gradually stiffens, becoming rigid just as the chocolated-cream melts completely.

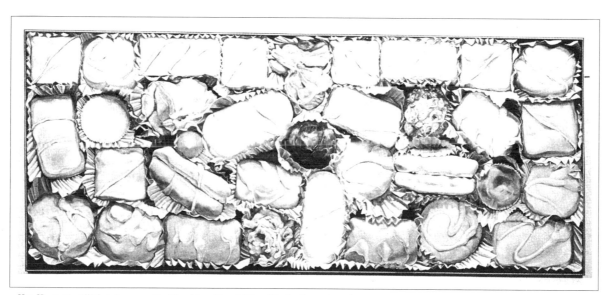

Kay Kurt, *For All Their Innocent Airs, They Know Exactly Where They're Going* (1968)

Raspberry Bonbons

KURT SCHWITTERS

Sweet jams drop down nights the fashionable lady.
In the form of a powder.
Bonanza sale (exhilarant, slimeiferous.)
A good whiff yond lady at her powdery shrine.
Long live the fashionable lady!
Long live the revolution!
Long live the Kaiser! (Drop down nights.)
Join together, all against all, for winds to boil over.
Shoot air! So   air   can   have
holes. Then long live the air with its holes,
the new holy shrine (slimeiferous in
the form of a powder.)
While I drop a cold monkey. (Good
whiffs.)

Translated by Jerome Rothenberg

The Test

IRIS MURDOCH

IN ENGLAND, my test of a really good
restaurant is whether or not it provides
bread and butter pudding.

Filloas De Padrón

CAMILO JOSÉ CELA

Ingredients
(for 6 persons)

Half-liter of milk
250 grams of flour
four eggs
50 grams of sugar

Procedure

1— Put the milk in a receptacle and add the flour, sugar, and eggs. Beat well. Let sit 30 minutes.

2— Fry them in a little butter in a small frying pan, adding spoonfuls (enough to cover the bottom of the pan), so that they are thin, and cook them on both sides. Put them in plates, adding sugar or a little Alcarria honey. Serve with a marc brandy.

Translated by Guy Bennett

Penitentiary Cookies

TOM RAWORTH

When we were living in San Francisco during the middle seventies Val worked for the city for a while. Soledad Carter, one of her workmates, gave us this recipe and I've enjoyed them whenever, since.

½ lb Sweet Butter

5 tablespoonsful Confectioner's Sugar

3 cups Flour

2 teaspoonsful Vanilla Essence

2 cups Chopped Pecans

¼ teaspoon Salt

Makes 3 dozen

Cream butter and sugar together. Work in flour, vanilla, pecans and salt into a firm dough with a wooden spoon. Divide into about 36 pieces in the shape of small cigars (they flatten while cooking). Place on ungreased baking sheet and bake for 15 minutes or until brown at 350° (Gas Mark 4).

"These are great cookies for open day at the penitentiary. Take your man a tin and they'll keep fresh until next visiting day." (S.C.)

Pain d'épice

(Gingerbread)

TOM AHERN

This is a recipe that has followed the path of immigration, from France to America, to East Lansing, Michigan, to be precise. It is one of the durable goods of memory.

It is an excellent tea bread and holiday gift.

My wife's splendid memory has cartwheels of the stuff laid out for slicing into portions, on the thick marble counter of a pâtisserie. From the windows one sees the Alps, the Mediterranean coast, the tidal bays of Normandy, the river chateaux, and Paris, example to the world.

INGREDIENTS

Mixture One: ½ cup honey

2 tablespoons anis

1 teaspoon cinnamon

½ teaspoon nutmeg

⅛ teaspoon ginger

⅛ teaspoon salt

optional 1–2 shots liqueur

(for my wife, who is a teetotaler by accident, this concluding shot seems optional; don't be misled)

Mixture Two:

2 cups flour

½ cup sugar

2 teaspoons baking soda

½–1 cup milk (not too runny!)

Let each mixture set in its separate bowl for 1 hour.

Mix together the two bowls.

Put batter in foil-lined pan.

Bake at 325° for about 45 min.

Let set 1 day and then taste.

Cakes

STACEY LEVINE

WANTING TO BE FULL, very full, because I was not full, I wanted to make a kind of plan, an arrangement. I might have known what that arrangement would be; I might have known all along; I already knew; I had only to extract it; a plan is mere logic; I went out, walking; the city, constructed around me, moved as I moved; I walked inside a building; I spoke to some people, and soon I had a job.

Having a job, I knew I would soon be full.

When away from my job, I began my plan; I used my money; I bought planks in many lengths; first planks, and later, paper; I carefully lined the shelves, lined them with sheets of paper, one on top of another; I built shelves with the planks; these ran the perimeters of my room, each shelf higher than the next, each carefully painted and paper-lined; it took some time; it took more than a day; and when I was done, all done with these shelves, I left my home. I went to my job.

When I returned from my job I saw the shelves, austere, clean. I wanted so much to be full; I was ready; there was no question that I wanted this, to be full. So after work, when I was ready, I went to the city; I moved quickly; I took a taxi; I bought many boxes of cakes, sheet cakes, tube cakes, each smooth on its top with the icing spread in strokes; each cake a different color; some were round, some square; there was no fanciness here, just cake and icing; these were simple cakes in boxes, cakes set within cardboard boxes upon cardboard trays and thin layers of paper; I bought the ones I chose, I ferried them home in a taxi; these cakes were dark brown, white, yellow; squares within squares; I went to buy more; they were to line my shelves; they lined my shelves. I hailed a taxi; I ferried them home in taxis; the day grew long; they would line my shelves, what a beautiful body I had; I was going to be full.

The shelves ran along my wall, across my window; the shelves were lined first with paper, then the boxes with their layers of cake. And I stood in my home now, looking at these cakes.

I stood looking at them. My plan was simple; I would begin to eat. I would put the cakes inside me; soon I would begin; soon I would eat and begin to be full; this would happen now; but gazing past the shelves, out the window, I saw something. I saw something on my property, something outside my house now; I saw a cat and dog.

A cat and dog had come. Though I could not know exactly when they had come because when I looked, they were already there. They might have been there on the pavement all along, even as I was building my shelves; as I looked now I saw them outside my home. They sat outside my window; they sat alongside each other, touching; they appeared to be at ease; I assumed they had come from elsewhere and then lay down here, though I had not seen them actually enter my property; in other words, I saw them now, though I had not seen exactly when or how they had arrived.

The cat was large and tall with long wide arms. The dog was tall with thinner arms. They reclined next to each other, touching. They were not starving, not ill; they sat outside the window as if it always had been their plan to do so; leaning on each other, completely still, they might have been resting; touching their arms together, they stared straight ahead as if in a photograph. The sun went down.

Their heads were very round and flat. The dog wore a cape made of plaid. Since I was standing away from the window, in the dark, they were probably unable to see me if they were watching, though I could not be sure if they were watching. A street lamp behind them cast their faces into shadow; they were each quite large and so were their heads. They were new here; in other words, I had never seen them in my neighborhood before.

As I had been planning to be full, I wanted it very badly, to get on with being full; I glanced at my cakes; I had not yet begun to open the boxes, which I would open with a clean knife; that was the plan; yet the cat and dog might have been watching, and I needed to leave for my job. I had to leave for my job; I left without cutting the white string that tied each box.

When I returned, I could not be at ease, not really, for, waiting to eat the cakes still, waiting since the day before or last week, I watched the dog and cat; I waited for them to leave, though they did not leave; it had been so long since I had conceived my plan, and from within my room I watched them as they watched me, though they might not have been watching me, and really, since they were so still, there was nothing for me to watch.

My plan had been to eat, to grow full, and to look at my body, full; I would look and never be able to have enough looking; I so wanted these things, yet the dog and cat were staring at me; I could not shake this disturbance; it would have been impossible, out of the question to watch myself as they were watching me; and still, I could not be positive that they were watching me, and so, for the moment, I tried to sleep.

It occurred to me in the night that they might have gone. I forgot my discomfort; I grew curious; outside, it was still damp, quiet night; I could not wait for the day; I used a flashlight; I aimed it into the darkness at them; I was not sure if they would have been there or gone so I used the flashlight; it was quite late,

and surely they would be gone. So I used the flashlight in order to see them gone.

But they lay together on the pavement; it was true, they were there still; I saw them, so motionless, their whiteness in the light beam; it seemed impossible, yet they were still there and remained there the night after that, too, their arms touching; I could have eaten the cake; I could have begun to be full, yet everything was worrisome; a disturbance; my discomfort grew; I wanted the cake, of course, and my mind would go back to this, the planks, the shelves, the layers of yellow, cream, and tan; how I wanted to be full; and soon I considered something new: that cake can harden at the edges and crack after a time. That cake can grow stale.

They were staring toward my house, toward me. Another day was ending; then, a thought came to me, a thought which actually had been with me for some time; a thought which must have occurred to me long before, though I did not know exactly when: that I could just smash those two.

I might have smashed them and the thought of smashing them did occur to me. They were my discomfort; they were both so strangely large after all and that was reason enough to smash them. But I had to leave for my job, and so I did. I put on my coat. I turned my head away from them as I passed; I really could not bear to look, and yet could not help glancing at their fur as I went past. I glanced at the red plaid of his cape over his fur.

Returning from work, I found that the cape caught my eye again; it made me feel ill. I entered my house, still waiting; I was waiting to eat the cakes, though now I felt ill. I watched those two from within my house, which was senseless; they hardly moved and only sat facing me, so still; they were quite senseless; so I looked at my shelves, and my cakes in the boxes instead.

I had bought the cakes with my money; I had bought them for me; I was now waiting to eat; I had been waiting so long and surely soon I should eat; how brilliant my body would have looked, would look, once I was full; and if in the future this were so, if my body was to become that much more beautiful, this, I knew, would be my happiness; then I would spend so very much time looking at my body, enjoying this, if only no one else would look as I was looking; if only I would have enough time to look without thinking someone else was looking; there was nothing but my body; yet the fact was now I felt ill.

Of course the thought of smashing them did occur to me. It seemed it would have been good to smash them and I thought I might have smashed them; yet the time in which I should have smashed them had passed; I should have smashed them immediately, when I first saw them, right away, without thinking; yet I had waited and so had forfeited the time in which I might have smashed them.

Then, I thought fewer times of smashing them; finally, I scarcely thought of it at all, because I was thinking carefully of the time in the future when I would already have eaten the cakes, the time when, on their shelves, they would be split, gouged, dug apart by my hands; their bright yellow insides turned over, noisy, exposed; that look of relief; I imagined it again: my body would be full.

I stood in my house, looking at the boxes, all tied shut; surely the cakes had not grown stale; cake inside a box can crack easily, I knew, but then I had been quite careful in handling the boxes all along; I looked out the window again; those two only reminded me now of themselves when I had first seen them: their air of intent. Yet they did nothing but stare as they lay on the pavement outside my house. And still, I could not be sure if they were staring at me.

Perhaps I had been baffled in those first moments of seeing them, and should have smashed them then without thinking; I probably would have, if it had occurred to me. But I only had been thinking then of being full, of my plan to grow full on the cakes and then to look at my body, full, for my body would show me forever its changes and naïveté and perfection as nothing else ever would.

But now, I needed to dress for my job; so I did, and then I left.

Returning from my job, I lay in bed. I turned to look at them outside, at their bodies reclining against each other, touching, at their blank expressions; they had not gone; their heads were so round, and at the moment, I felt quite ill.

Pumpkin Pie

KEITH WALDROP

To make a pumpkin pie, you need first of all a pumpkin. This means it can be made only in season, since what comes in cans is something else.

Cut the pumpkin in two or more pieces, removing the seeds. Boil or bake these pieces until soft, then with a spoon scrape the meat off the rind. Four to six cups of the meat will make one pie.

The meat varies from pumpkin to pumpkin but will probably be stringy. Put it through a blender, adding (per pie) the following:

½ teaspoon salt
1 cup brown sugar (or to taste)
1 tablespoon blackstrap molasses
¼ teaspoon ground cloves
2 teaspoons ground cinnamon
the juice of half a lemon
1 tablespoon of orange curaçao
1 tablespoon Worcestershire sauce
2 eggs

When all this is blended together, it should be just liquid enough to pour into the shell. If the mixture seems too dry, add apple cider—preferably old and turning cider.

Pour into a pie shell that has been par-baked for 5 minutes at 400 degrees. Sprinkle the top of the pie with either nutmeg or grated orange peel.

Bake at 400 degrees for 15 minutes, then turn oven to 350 degrees and bake for another 20 minutes. When it is done, the edges should look solid while the center is still somewhat viscous.

Let the pie cool. Top with whipped cream.

This pumpkin pie is not absolutely traditional, but could become so.

Wayne Thiebaud, *Pie Counter* (1963)

Pies

KIER PETERS

In the middle of a yard stands a woman with a large straw garden hat. She points at GRANDMA, *sitting on a couch.*

MOTHER: Now sit down there very nicely and be out of the way!

GRANDMA: What?

MOTHER: Sit down very nice.

GRANDMA: [*Looking about*] Where is the house?

MOTHER: [*Busying herself*] We will build one around you and me one day.

GRANDMA: Who?

MOTHER: The man whom I may marry then.

GRANDMA: Who?

MOTHER: You'll know him when he comes.

GRANDMA: I will?

MOTHER: And everyone will be happy in the end. [*Taking a pie out of the stove.*] As soon as it cools down I'll cut you a slice.

GRANDMA: What kind?

MOTHER: You know I've forgotten what I put in.

GRANDMA: Because I don't like cherry or apricot.

MOTHER: I don't think it's cherry and I doubt I've made apricot since it's something I've never done.

GRANDMA: And I don't like apple nor blueberry nor rhubarb mince banana raisin or chocolate.

MOTHER: Gee I don't know what to say it might be one of those it just might.

GRANDMA: Nor lemon nor lime nor peach. I completely hate peach.

MOTHER: Well Grandma what do you like?

GRANDMA: [*Screwing up her face*] I forgot.

MOTHER: [*Putting down the pie*] I'm not going to serve it then besides it wasn't really a pie. It's a cake.

GRANDMA: I like cake.

Memories, Cigars, Liquors and Late Night Snacks

Larry Rivers, *Webster and Cigars* (1964–66)

⊗

The Dinner Party

ROBERT WALSER

IT WAS a delightful dinner party. There was plenty of mustard, and the whole works was accompanied by the finest wine. The soup was admittedly a bit thick, and the fish contributed nothing to the entertainment, but no one took it amiss. Over the table poured sauces that put us in raptures, me more than anyone—I was fairly glowing, practically perished with pleasure. A downright tough, hearty roast ensured that our teeth were given a proper workout. I tucked right in. Among other things, a duck was served. The lady of the house kept laughing up her sleeve, and the servants sought to encourage us by clapping us on the shoulders.

The cheese was also delectable. When we stood up, a cigar flew into each and every mouth, a cup of coffee into each and every hand. Every plate vanished the instant it was emptied. We waded up to our necks in witty conversation. The liqueur made us swim in a more beautiful age, and when a songstress performed, we were simply beside ourselves. After we'd recovered, a poet deeply moved us with his verses. At any rate, the beer kept right on flowing, and all and sundry enjoyed themselves.

One of the guests was frozen. All attempts to bring him to life were in vain. The ladies' dresses were magnificent; they revealed quite a lot, thus leaving nothing to be desired. One man attracted attention by wearing a laurel wreath—no one begrudged him this. A second polemicized until he found himself alone, since no one was willing to put up with him. A pair of musicians played Mendelssohn, to which all attentively gave ear. Someone pulled off a great many shirt-fronts and collars and noses. The joke was a bit crude, but no one thought anything about it. The manager of a theater fantasized about till-filling dramas, a publisher about epoch-making publications.

In parting I slipped the butler a hundred-franc tip. He returned it with the remark that he was accustomed to better wages. I asked him to be content with less just this once. Outside a car awaited me, which then whisked me away, and so off I drove, and no doubt am still doing so to this day.

Translated by Susan Berofsky

MEMORIES, CIGARS, LIQUORS AND LATE NIGHT SNACKS

Frank Majore, *The Temptation of Saint Anthony* (1984)

Cigarren (elemental)

Cigarren
Ci
garr
ren
Ce
i
ge
a
err
err
e
en
Ce
CeI
CeIGe
CeIGeA
CeIGeAErr
CeIGeAErrEr
CeIGeAErrErr
CeIGeAErrErr
ErrEEn
EEn
En
Ce
i
ge
a
err
err
e
en
Ci
garr
ren
Cigarren (last line sung)

Kurt Schwitters

Translated by Jerome Rothenberg & Pierre Joris

Late Night Celebration

THOMAS MANN

"THE HOUR is at hand," said he, and sent for the wine-card. He put on a horn-rimmed pince-nez, the nose-piece of which rode high up on his forehead, and ordered champagne, three bottles of Mumm & Co., *Cordon rouge,* extra dry, with *petits fours,* toothsome cone-shaped little dainties in lace frills, covered with coloured frosting and filled with chocolate and *pistache* cream. Frau Stöhr licked her fingers after them. Herr Albin nonchalantly removed the wire from the first bottle, and let the mushroom-shaped cork pop to the ceiling; elegantly he conformed to the ritual, holding the neck of the bottle wrapped in a serviette as he poured. The noble foam bedewed the cloth. Every glass rang as the guests saluted, then drank the first one empty at a draught, electrifying their digestive organs with the ice-cold, prickling, perfumed liquid. Every eye sparkled. The game had come to an end, no one troubled to take cards or gains from the table. They gave themselves over to a blissful *far niente,* enlivened by scraps of conversation in which, out of sheer high spirits, no one hung back. They uttered thoughts that in the thinking had seemed primevally fresh and beautiful, but in the saying somehow turned lame, stammering, indiscreet, a perfect gallimaufry, calculated to arouse the scorn of any sober onlooker. The audience, however, took no offence, all being in much the same irresponsible condition. Even Frau Magnus's ears were red and she admitted that she felt "as though life were running through her"—which Herr Magnus seemed not-over-pleased to hear. Hermine Kleefeld leaned against Herr Albin's shoulder as she held her glass to be filled. Peeperkorn conducted the Bacchanalian rout with his long-fingered gestures, and summoned additional supplies: coffee followed the champagne, "Mocha double," with fresh rounds of "bread," and pungent liqueurs: apricot brandy, chartreuse, *crème de vanille,* and maraschino for the ladies. Later there appeared marinated *filets* of fish, and beer; lastly tea, both Chinese and chamomile, for those who had done with champagne and liqueurs and did not care to return to a sound wine, as Mynheer himself did; he, Frau Chauchat, and Hans Castorp working back after midnight to a Swiss red wine. Mynheer Peeperkorn, genuinely thirsty, drank down glass after glass of the simple, effervescent drink.

Translated by H.T. Lowe-Porter

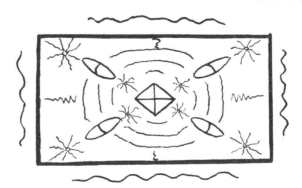

Giuseppe Steiner, *Coffee After Midnight,* (1923)

This is Just to Say

WILLIAM CARLOS WILLIAMS

I have eaten
the plums
that were in
the icebox

and which
you were probably
saving
for breakfast

Forgive me
they were delicious
so sweet
and so cold

Roy Lichtenstein, *The Tablet* (1966)

SOURCES AND PERMISSIONS

Literature

Alfau, Felipe. from *Chromos* (Elmwood Park, Illinois: Dalkey Archive Press, 1990), pp. 124–129. Copyright ©1990 by Felipe Alfau. Reprinted by permission of Dalkey Archive Press.

Achleitner, Friedrich. "The Good Soup," from *The Vienna Group: Six Major Austrian Poets.* Translated by Rosmarie Waldrop and Harriett Watts (Barrytown, New York: Station Hill Press, 1985), pp. 66–68. Copyright ©1985 by Rosmarie Waldrop and Harriett Watts and Station Hill Press. Reprinted by permission of the translators.

Beckett, Samuel. from *Watt* (New York: Grove Press, 1959), pp. 87–88. Copyright ©1953 by Samuel Beckett. Used by permission of Grove/Atlantic, Inc.

Biely, Andrey. from *St. Petersburg*, translated by John Cournos (New York: Grove Press, 1959), pp. 189–190. Copyright ©1959, 1987 by Grove Press, Inc. Used by permission of Grove/Atlantic Inc.

Bjørneboe, Jens. from *The Bird Lovers*, translated by Frederick Wasser (Los Angeles: Sun & Moon Press, 1994), pp. 22–23. Copyright ©1966 by Jens Bjørneboe; translation ©1994 by Frederick Wasser. Reprinted by permission of Sun & Moon Press/The Contemporary Arts Educational Project, Inc.

Blackburn, Paul. "A Dull Poem," from *The Collected Poems of Paul Blackburn* (New York: Persea Books, 1985), pp. 229–231. Coyright ©1955, 1960, 1961, 1966, 1967, 1968, 1969, 1970, 1971, 1972, 1975, 1978, 1980, 1983, 1985 by Joan Blackburn. Reprinted by permission of Persea Books.

Borgen, Johan. from *Lillelord*, translated by Elizabeth Brown Moen and Ronald E. Peterson (New York: New Directions, 1982), pp. 118–120. Copyright ©1982 by Elizabeth Brown Moen and Ronald E. Peterson. Reprinted by permission of New Directions.

Bowen, Elizabeth. from *Eva Trout* (London: Jonathan Cape, 1969), p. 182. Copyright ©1968 by Elizabeth Bowen. Reprinted by permission of Alfred A. Knopf, Inc.

Corbett, William. "Bowl of Progresso Minestrone," from *Arshile*, no. 1 (1993). Copyright ©1993 by 96 Tears Press. Reprinted by permission of the author.

Coronel Urtecho, José. "A Text on Corn," from *Prosa* (San José, Costa Rica: Editorial Universitaria Centroaméricana, 1972). Copyright ©1972 by EDUCA, Centroamérica; translation by Gilbert Alter Gilbert, ©Sun & Moon Press, 1994.

de Chazal, Malcolm. Selections from *Plastic Sense*, translated by Irving J. Weiss (New York: Herder & Herder, 1971). Copyright ©1971 by Herder and Herder, Inc.

Desani, G. V. from *All About H. Hatterr* (New Paltz, New York: McPherson & Co., 1986), p. 249. Copyright ©1970, 1972, 1986 by G. V. Desani. Reprinted by permission of the author.

di Lampedusa, Giuseppe. from *The Leopard*, translated by Archibald Colquhoun (New York: Pantheon, 1960), pp. 96–97. Copyright ©1960 in the English translation by William Collins Sons & Co., Ltd. London and Pantheon Books, Inc. Reprinted by permission of Pantheon Books, Inc., a division of Random House, Inc.

García Márquez, Gabriel. from *One Hundred Years of Solitude*, translated by Gregory Rabassa. (New York: Harper & Row, 1970), pp. 65–66. Translation copyright ©1970 by Harper & Row, Publishers, Inc. Reprinted by permission of HarperCollins Publishers, Inc.

George, Charley. "peanuts discover each other as butter" from *Sunday's Ending Too Soon* (Los Angeles: Sun & Moon Press, 1993), p. 49. Copyright ©1990, 1993 by Kathi George. Reprinted by permission of Sun & Moon Press/The Contemporary Arts Educational Project, Inc.

Gunnarsson, Gunnar. from *Ships in the Sky* (Indianapolis: The Bobbs-Merrill Company, 1938), p. 279. Copyright ©1938 by The Bobs-Merrill Company.

Hawkes, John. from *The Blood Oranges* (New York: New Directions, 1971), pp. 50–52. Copyright ©1970, 1971 by John Hawkes. Reprinted by permission of New Directions.

Hemingway, Ernest. from *The Sun Also Rises* (New York: Charles Scribner's Sons, 1954), p. 76. Copyright ©1926 by Charles Scribner's Sons; renewed ©1954 by Ernest Hemingway. Reprinted by permission of Scribner's, an imprint of Simon & Schuster.

Ionesco, Eugène. from "The Slough" in *The Colonel's Photograph and Other Stories*, translated by Jean Stewart (New York: Grove Press, 1969), pp. 104–105. Copyright ©1967 by Faber and Faber Limited. Reprinted by permission of Georges Borchardt Inc.

Joyce, James. from *Ulysses* (New York: Vintage Books [Random House], 1961), p. 55. Copyright ©1914, 1918 by Margaret Caroline Anderson. Copyright renewed, 1942, 1946 by Nora Joseph Joyce. Copyright ©1934, by Modern Library Inc. Copyright renewed ©1961 by Lucia and George Joyce.

Kafka, Franz. from *The Metamorphosis*, translated by Willa and Edwin Muir (New York: Schocken Books, 1968), pp. 51 and 53. Copyright ©1948 by Schocken Books Inc., New York. Reprinted by permission of Schocken Books, a division of Random House, Inc.

Lawrence, Jerome and Robert E. Lee. from *Auntie Mame* (New York: The Vanguard Press [Random House], 1957). Copyright ©1957 by Jerome Lawrence and Robert E. Lee. Reprinted by permission of the authors.

Levine, Stacey. "Cakes" from *My Horse and Other Stories* (Los Angeles: Sun & Moon Press, 1993), pp. 41–46. Copyright ©1993 by Stacey Levine. Reprinted by permission of Sun & Moon Press/The Contemporary Arts Educational Project, Inc.

Lowry, Malcolm. from *Under the Volcano* (Philadelphia: J. B. Lippincott Company, 1947), pp. 90–91. Copyright ©1947 by Malcolm Lowry. Copyright renewed 1975 by Margerie Lowry. Reprinted by permission of HarperCollins Publishers, Inc.

Mann, Thomas. from *The Magic Mountain*, translated by H. T. Lowe-Porter (New York: Alfred A. Knopf, 1944, 1967), pp. 570–571. Copyright ©1927 by Alfred A. Knopf, Inc.; renewed copyright ©1952 by Thomas Mann. Reprinted by permission of Alfred A. Knopf, Inc.

Marinetti, F. T. and family. from *La Cucina Futurista*. (Milan: Longanesi & Co., 1986), p. 205. Copyright ©1986. Translation ©1994 by Guy Bennett in *The Sun & Moon Guide to Eating Through Literature and Art*.

Mathews, Harry. "Country Cooking from Central France: Roast Boned Rolled Stuffed Shoulder of Lamb (Farce Double)," from *Country Cooking and Other Stories* (Providence: Burning Deck, 1980), pp. 9–38. Copyright ©1980 by Harry Mathews. Reprinted by permission of Burning Deck Press.

Nabokov, Vladimir. from *Ada or Ardor: A Family Chronicle* (New York: McGraw-Hill Company, 1969), pp. 249–250. Copyright ©1990 by The Estate of Vladimir Nabokov. Reprinted by permission of Vintage Books, a Division of Random House, Inc.

Pavić, Milorad. from *Dictionary of the Khazars*, translated by Christina Pribićević-Zorić (New York: Alfred A. Knopf, 1988), pp. 39–41. Copyright ©1988 by Alfred A. Knopf, Inc. Reprinted by permission of Alfred A. Knopf, Inc.

Perreault, John. "The Big Cheese," from *Hotel Death and Other Tales* (Los Angeles: Sun & Moon Press, 1989), pp. 140–150. Copyright ©1989 by John Perreault. Reprinted by permission of Sun & Moon Press/The Contemporary Arts Educational Project, Inc.

Peters, Kier. from *The Confirmation* (Los Angeles: Sun & Moon Press, 1993), pp. 7–8. Copyright ©Kier Peters, 1993. Reprinted by permission of Sun & Moon Press/The Contemporary Arts Educations Project, Inc.

Piñera, Virgilio. "Meat," from *Cold Tales*, translated by Mark Schafer (Hygiene, Colorado: Eridanos Press, 1988), pp. 9–12. Copyright ©1987 by Estela Piñera; translation ©1987 by Mark Schafer. Reprinted by permission of Marsilio Publishers.

Pinter, Harold. from *The Caretaker & The Dumb Waiter* (New York: Grove Press, 1961), pp. 86–87. Copyright ©1960, 1988 by Harold Pinter. Used by permission of Grove/Atlantic, Inc.

Pynchon, Thomas. from *Gravity's Rainbow* (New York: The Viking Press, 1973), pp. 115–117. Copyright ©1973 by Thomas Pynchon. Used by permission of Viking Penguin, a division of Penguin Books USA, Inc.

Proust, Marcel. from *Swann's Way*, translated by Guy Bennett. Copyright ©1994, Guy Bennett. Reprinted by permission of Sun & Moon Press/The Contemporary Arts Educational Project, Inc.

Ronk, Martha. "Peas" in *Ribot: A Subversion*, No. 1 (1993), p. 98. Copyright ©1993 by CONS. Reprinted by permission of the author.

Roubaud, Jacques. from *The Great Fire of London*, translated by Dominic Di Bernardi (Elmwood Park, Illinois: Dalkey Archive Press, 1991), pp. 200–202. Copyright ©1991 by Dominic Di Bernardi. Reprinted by permission of Dalkey Archive Press.

Sandemose, Aksel. from *A Fugitive Crosses His Tracks*, translated by Eugene Gay-Tifft (New York: Alfred A. Knopf, 1936), p. 73. Copyright ©1936 by Alfred A. Knopf, Inc. Reprinted by permission of Alfred A. Knopf, Inc.

Sarduy, Severo. from *From Cuba with a Song*, translated by Suzanne Jill Levine (Los Angeles, Sun & Moon Press, 1994), p. 48. Copyright ©1994, 1972 by Suzanne Jill Levine. Reprinted by permission of Sun & Moon Press/The Contemporary Arts Educational Project, Inc.

Schulz, Bruno. from "Tailor's Dummies," from *The Complete Fiction of Bruno Schulz* (New York: Walker and Company, 1989), pp. 25–26. Copyright ©1989 by Ellia Podstolski-Schulz. Reprinted with permission from Walker and Company, 435 Hudson Street, New York, NY 10014, 1-800-289-2553. All rights reserved.

Schwitters, Kurt. "Raspberry Bonbons" and "Cigarren" from *ppppppp: Poems Performance Pieces Proses Plays Poetics*, edited and translated by Jerome Rothenberg and Pierre Joris (Philadelphia: Temple University Press, 1993), pp. 36, 40.

Sorrentino, Gilbert. from *Misterioso* (Elmwood Park, Illinois: Dalkey Archive Press, 1989). Copyright ©1989 by Gilbert Sorrentino. Reprinted by permission of the author and publisher.

Stein, Gertrude. "Lunch" and "Sugar" from *Tender Buttons* (Los Angeles: Sun & Moon Press, 1991), pp. 44–46, 48–49.

Strindberg, August. from *The Natives of Hemsö,* translated by Arvid Paulson (New York: Liveright, 1965), p. 67. Copyright ©1965 by Arvid Paulson.

Swewc, Piotr. from *Annihilation,* translated by Ewa Hryniewicz-Yarbrough (Normal, Illinois: Dalkey Archive Press, 1993), pp. 13–14. Reprinted by permission of the publisher.

Tanizaki, Junichirō. from *The Makioka Sisters*, translated by Edward G. Seidensticker (New York: Everyman's Library [Alfred A. Knopf], 1993). Copyright ©1957 by Alfred A. Knopf. Reprinted by permission of Alfred A. Knopf, Inc.

Van Vechten, Carl. from *Peter Whiffle* (New York: Alfred A. Knopf, 1923), p. 127 and 169. Copyright ©1922 by Alfred A. Knopf, Inc.

Walser, Robert. "Food (1)" and "The Dinner Party," reprinted from *Masquerade and Other Stories*, translated by Susan Bernofsky (Baltimore: The Johns Hopkins University Press, 1990), pp. 46–47 and 111–112. Copyright ©1990 by The Johns Hopkins University Press. Reprinted by permission of The Johns Hopkins University Press.

Waugh, Evelyn. from *A Handful of Dust* (New York: New Directions, 1945), p. 115. Copyright ©1934 by Little Brown & Company. Reprinted by permission of Little Brown & Company.

Weinstein, Jeff. "A Jean-Marie Cookbook," from *Contemporary American Fiction* (Washington, D.C.: Sun & Moon Press, 1983), pp. 183–204. Copyright ©1978 by Jeff Weinstein. Reprinted by permission of the author and Sun & Moon Press/The Contemporary Arts Educational Project, Inc.

Welty, Eudora. from *Losing Battles* (New York: Random House, 1970), pp. 190–191. Copyright ©1970 by Eudora Welty. Reprinted by permission of Random House, Inc.

Williams, William Carlos. "This Is Just to Say" from *The Collected Poems of William Carlos Williams*, Volume I (New York: New Directions, 1986), p. 372. Copyright ©1917, 1921 by The Four Seas Company; ©1934 by The Objectivist Press; ©1935 by The Alcestis Press; ©1936 by Ronald Lane Latimer; ©1938 by New Directions Publishing Corporation; ©1930, 1931, 1933, 1935, 1937, 1938, 1939, 1951, 1952 by William Carlos Williams; ©1957, 1966, 1974 by Florence H. Williams; ©1982, 1986 by William Eric Williams and Paul H. Williams; ©1986 by A. Walton Litz and Christopher MacGowan. Reprinted by permission of New Directions.

Wolfe, Thomas. from *Look Homeward, Angel* (New York: Charles Scribner's Sons, 1929). Copyright ©1929 by Charles Scribner's Sons; copyright renewed ©1957 Edward C. Aswell, as Administrator, C.T.A. of the Estate of Thomas Wolfe and/or Fred W. Wolfe. Reprinted with permission of Scribner's, an imprint of Simon & Schuster.

Woolf, Virginia. from *Mrs. Dalloway* (New York: Harcourt, Brace & World, Inc., 1953), pp. 251–252. Copyright ©1925 Harcourt Brace & World, Inc.; copyright ©1953 renewed by Leonard Woolf. Reprinted by permission of the publisher.

Antin, Eleanor. *A Refusal* from *The 8 Temptations, 1972*. Color photograph. Courtesy the artist.

Arman. *Four O'Clock Pyramid*, 1977 (20 × 20 × 20 inches, accumulation of tea pots. Courtesy A R S (Artists Rights Society). Copyright ©1995 Artists Rights Society (A R S), New York A D A G P, Paris.

Baldessari, John. *Banquet*, 1988 (73 ¼ × 144 ½ inches, Black and white photographs with vinyl paint; mounted on board). Courtesy Margo Leavin Gallery, Los Angeles. Private Collection, Courtesy of Masimo Martino S.A.-Lugano. Photographer: Douglas M. Parker, Los Angeles.

Barnes, Djuna. Untitled drawing of "Pot-au-Feu." Courtesy Sun & Moon Press, Los Angeles.

Beaton, Cecil. *Edith Sitwell Taking Tea in Bed*, 1927. Courtesy Sotheby's, London.

Botero, Fernando. *Onions*, 1974 (54 ½ × 60 ½ inches, oil on canvas). Collection of Mr. and Mrs. Leigh B. Block, Chicago. Courtesy V A G A, New York. © 1994 Fernando Botero/V A G A, New York.

Braque, Georges. *Blackfish*, 1942 (13 × 21 ½ inches, oil on canvas). Collection: Musée National d'Art Moderne, Centre Georges Pompidou, Paris.

Broodthaers, Marcel. *La Soupe de Daguerre*, 1976 (21 × 20 ½ inches, Twelve color-coupler prints on paper). Courtesy of Multiples/Marion Goodman Gallery, New York.

Cadmus, Paul. *Apple Peeler*, 1959 (15 × 7 inches, egg tempera on Whatman board). Collection: Modern Art Museum of Fort Worth, Texas.

Cage, John in unattributed photograph, *John Cage and Gianni Sassi in Milan*, 1988.

Caulfield, Patrick. *Still Life: Autumn Fashion*, 1978 (61 × 76 cm, acrylic on canvas). Courtesy Walker Art Gallery.

Cornell, Joseph. *A Pantry Ballet for Jacques Offenbach*, 1942 (10 ½ × 18 × 6 inches, construction in paper, plastic, and wood). Collection: Mr. and Mrs. Richard L. Feigen, New York.

Dali, Salvador. *Basket of Bread*, 1926 (12 ½ × 12 ½ inches, oil on panel). Collection: The Salvador Dali Museum, Saint Petersburg, Florida. Copyright ©1994 The Savador Dali Museum, Inc.

Depero, Fortunato. from *Numero unico futurista Campari* 1931 (Published by the Author).

Dickinson, Preston. *Still Life with Yellow Green Chair*. Courtesy Ferdinand Howald Collection, The Columbus Gallery of Fine Arts

Imes, Birney. *Rabbit hunters, Lowndes County, Mississippi 1980* (Black and white photograph).

Knott, Herbie. *Gilbert & George at the Market Café, London 1987*. Courtesy Anthony D'Offay Gallery, London and Gilbert & George.

Kuniyoshi, Yasuo. *Boy Stealing Fruit*, 1921 (oil on canvas). Courtesy Ferdinand Howald Collection, The Columbus Gallery of Fine Arts.

Kurt, Kay. *For All Their Innocent Airs, They Know Exactly Where They're Going*, 1968 (60 × 144 inches, oil on canvas). Collection: Roy R. Neuburger, New York. Photograph: Jay Cantor.

Lichtenstein, Roy. *Mustard on White*, 1963 (24 × 32 inches, magna on plexiglass). Courtesy the artist.
    Tablet, 1966 (30 × 22 inches, pencil and tusche). Collection: Mrs. Richard Selle, New York. Courtesy the artist. Copyright © Roy Lichtenstein.

Luks, George B. *The Butcher Boy*, (oil on canvas). Collection unknown.

Magritte, René. *Portrait [Le Portrait]*, 1935 (28 ⅞ × 19 ⅞ inches, oil on canvas). Collection: Museum of Modern Art, New York. Gift of Kay Sage Tanguy © Courtesy Museum of Modern Art.
    Pleasure, 1926 (29 ½ × 39 ⅜ inches, oil on canvas). Collection: Gerrit Lansing, New York.

Majore, Frank. *The Temptation of Saint Anthony*, 1984 (20 × 24 inches, Cibachrome print). Photographer: Marvin Heiferman, New York. Courtesy New Strategies, Los Angeles.

Messerli, Douglas. *Eggs*, 1978 (5 ⅜ × 2 ½ inches, paper collage). Courtesy the artist.

Murphy, Gerald. *Cocktail*, 1927 (28 × 29 inches, oil on canvas). Collection Mrs. Philip Barry.

Nelson, Jud. *Holos/Series 5 [tea bags]*, 1978 (1 × 2 ¼ × 6 inches, white Carrara marble). Photograph: Bevan Davies. Courtesy the artist.

Oldenburg, Claes. *Viandes*, 1964 (37 × 73 × 16 inches, plaster, canvas, painted with tempera, porcelain plates, marble top base). Collection: Museum Boymans van Beuningen, Rotterdam. Courtesy the artist. Photograph by Attilio Maranzano, Rome.

...nheim, Meret. *Cannibal feast*, 1959 (photograph). Courtesy Galerie Daniel Cordier, Paris, 1959.

...rker, Bart. *Tomatoe Picture,* 1977 (10 × 13 inches, chromogenic-development [Ektacolor] print). Collection of the artist. Courtesy of the Visual Studies Workshop, Rochester.

Picasso, Pablo. *Glass of Absinthe*, 1914 (8 ½ × 6 ½ inches; diameter at base 2 ½ inches, painted bronze with silver spoon). Collection The Museum of Modern Art, New York, gift of Mrs. Bertram Smith.

Ramos, Mel. *Val Veeta*, 1965 (61 × 70 inches, oil on canvas). Courtesy Louis K. Meisel Gallery, New York.

Ray, Man. *Mr. Knife and Miss Fork*, 1944 (13 ½ × 9 ¾ inches, mixed media object). Collection of Jules Brassner, Florida.

Rivers, Larry. *Webster and Cigars*, 1964–66 (13 ¼ × 16 × 13 ¼ inches, construction). Photograph O.E. Nelson. Courtesy VAGA, New York. © 1994 Larry Rivers/VAGA, New York.

Rosenquist, James. *Silhouette II*, 1962 (41 × 47 inches, oil on canvas). Photograph Rudolph Burckhardt. Courtesy VAGA, New York. © 1994 James Rosenquist/VAGA, New York.

Ruscha, Edward. *Jelly*, 1964 (10 ½ × 12 inches, ink on paper). Courtesy the artist.

Sander, August. *Pastry Cook, Cologne 1928* (Ektachrome). Courtesy August Sander Archiv/Stiftung City-Treff, Cologne; VG Bild-Kunst, Bonn 1994.

Schohin, Wladimir. *Still life*, ca. 1907 (6 ¾ × 9 ⅞ inches, modern Cibachrome print from original autochrome). Collection: Amartörfotografklubben, Helsinki.

Skoglund, Sandy. *Luncheon Meat on a Counter*, 1978. (22 × 28 inches, Cibachrome). Courtesy Los Angeles County Museum of Art. Copyright ©1978 by Sandy Skoglund.

Spoerri, Daniel. *Marcel Duchamp's Dinner*, 1964 (24 ⅞ × 21 ⅛ × 8 ¼ inches, cutlery, dishes, and napkins mounted on wood). Collection: Arman, Nice.

Steiner, Giuseppe. "Caffè dopo mezzanotte" ["Coffee After Midnight"] from *Drawn States of Mind,* translated by Guy Bennett (Los Angeles: Sun & Moon Press, 1994), p. 26. Reprinted by permission of the publisher.

Thiebaud, Wayne. *Pie Counter*, 1963 (30 × 36 inches, oil on canvas). Whitney Museum of American Art, New York, Larry Aldrich Foundation Fund. Photograph: Geoffrey Clements.

Unattributed photograph [couple with vegetables].

Warhol, Andy. *4 Campbell's Soup Cans*, 1962 (oil on canvas). Collection: Mr. and Mrs. Leo Castelli. Photograph: Rudolph Burckhardt. Courtesy the Andy Warhol Foundation, New York.

Weston, Edward. *Hot Coffee, Mojave Desert,* 1937 (photograph). Copyright ©1981 Center for Creative Photography, Arizona Board of Regents.

Wood, Grant. *Dinner for Threshers*, 1933 (17 ¾ × 26 ¾ inches, pencil and gouache on paper). Collection: Whitney Museum of American Art, New York.

The text of this book is set in Monotype
Perpetua, designed by Eric Gill in 1925–30.
Gill's first typeface design, Perpetua was drawn
for a privately printed translation of *The Passion
of Perpetua and Felicity,* made by Walter Shrewing
in 1928 and from which it took its name. The
italic, originally called Felicity, was completed
in 1930.

Other typefaces include Lucian Bernhard's
Bernhard Tango (selection titles) and Dennis
Ortiz-Lopez' Miehle Classic Condensed (au-
thors' names).

Typeset by Guy Bennett.